"PLAY BALL!"

If you like baseball, then you know *anything* can happen after those two magic words! Whether it's an amazing play by a talented star, a ball that takes off after a bad hop, or a team that comes through when you least expect it to, the game is full of surprises! Those amazing moments—the good, the bad, and the funny—are captured in this book. On top of that, you'll find lots of pictures of the very best . . .

STRANGE AND AMAZING BASEBALL STORIES!

Books by Bill Gutman

GREAT MOMENTS IN PRO FOOTBALL
REFRIGERATOR PERRY
STRANGE AND AMAZING BASEBALL STORIES
STRANGE AND AMAZING FOOTBALL STORIES
STRANGE AND AMAZING WRESTLING STORIES

Available from ARCHWAY Paperbacks

Sports Illustrated

STRANGE & AMAZING
BASEBALL STORIES

Bill Gutman

AN ARCHWAY PAPERBACK
Published by POCKET BOOKS • NEW YORK

Photographs courtesy of *Sports Illustrated:* Jacqueline Duvoisin pages 5, 65; John Iacono page 97; Walter Iooss Jr. page 40; Fred Kaplan page 31; Anthony Neste page 8; Herb Scharfman page 52; Tony Triolo page 71. Photographs on pages 23, 56, 62, 91, 112 courtesy of AP/Wide World Photos. Photographs on pages 10, 37, 87, 89 courtesy of National Baseball Library, Cooperstown, N.Y.

AN ARCHWAY PAPERBACK *Original*

An Archway Paperback published by
POCKET BOOKS, a division of Simon & Schuster, Inc.
1230 Avenue of the Americas, New York, N.Y. 10020

ISBN: 0-671-61125-9

First Archway Paperback printing March 1987

10 9 8 7 6 5 4 3 2 1

Introduction

On the surface, baseball is a very simple game. The pitcher throws the ball toward home plate and the batter tries to hit it. That has been the essence of the professional game since it began well over 100 years ago. Yet if you account for all the different things that can happen during a ball game, baseball becomes perhaps the most complex sport of them all.

There is an old expression that baseball is so difficult because the batter has to hit a round ball with a round bat and the object is to hit it square. That may be a play on words, but there is some truth to it. Hall of Famer Ted Williams, among others, always contended that hitting a baseball was the most difficult skill to master in all of sports. That may well be true. Yet there have been many great hitters in the history of the game, as well as a wealth of great pitchers. Add to that the great fielders, exciting base runners, top strategists, and the psychological battles that are fought every game, and it's easy to understand why anything can happen on the diamond.

But even all of that doesn't quite make baseball the great game that it is. There are also the many and varied individuals who have crossed the playing fields of America down through the years. It is these personalities who have shaped the game and given it its great traditions. They have also contributed to and created the great moments, as well as the funny and strange events that have occurred during the seasons of play.

Strange and Amazing Baseball Stories will look at some of the unusual happenings over the years involving both the great and the ordinary player. The book will prove, once and for all, that you can never predict what will happen at the ballpark. The game of baseball may begin with the pitcher throwing the ball toward the batter. But along the way that little white baseball can take some pretty unexpected twists and turns. As funny as the stories sound, as strange as they may be, as amazing to believe, each and every one has something in common. They really happened.

STRANGE & AMAZING
BASEBALL STORIES

Chapter 1

ONCE IN A LIFETIME

In all the years professional baseball has been played, certain events and occurrences stand out as once-in-a-lifetime happenings. Some are simply unusual, some humorous, while others border on the fantastic, and a few are even tragic. But no matter the tone, all have a common link. They have happened just once and may never happen again. The following anecdotes are just some of these strange, funny, and amazing once-in-a-lifetime events that have become a permanent part of baseball folklore.

Every player remembers his first big league at bat. It's a moment forever etched in his memory, something he'll never forget. But for Billy Herman of the Chicago Cubs, the memory isn't complete. He can only recall one-half of his major league debut at the plate.

Ultimately one of the finest players of his generation, Herman compiled a .304 lifetime batting average from 1931 to 1947. But when the Cubs called him up from the minors in the middle of the 1931 season, the twenty-two-year-old rookie was anxious to make a big impression.

Digging in against Cincinnati hurler Si Johnson, Billy got his pitch and swung from the heels. He heard the crack of the bat on the ball . . . but that's all he heard. He had fouled the ball off the ground behind the plate with tremendous force. The ball then bounced up and smacked Billy in the back of the head, knocking him out cold.

So before his first at bat in the major leagues could be completed, Billy Herman was being carried from the field on a stretcher. He would always remember his first at bat, all right—at least the part before the lights went out!

A debut of another kind was made by Hoyt Wilhelm, the brilliant knuckleball relief pitcher who started his career with the New York Giants in 1952. Wilhelm's knuckler kept him in the majors until 1972, when he was nearly forty-nine years old, and in that time he made more mound appearances than any other pitcher in baseball history.

But it was his debut at the plate that must have made the Giants wonder if Wilhelm was actually a slugging outfielder disguised as a pitcher. His first time up as a major league batter, Wilhelm took a big cut, and he belted one over the left field fence for a home run! A couple of innings later he was up again and showed everyone it was no fluke. This time he hit a shot into the gap between the outfielders and legged it into a triple. You can't start much better than that.

Perhaps the Giants were already thinking they had another Babe Ruth on their hands (the Babe started out as a pitcher before his great bat forced his conversion to the outfield). Luckily, the Giants didn't make any hasty decisions. Before long, Wilhelm settled into a groove as a typical light-hitting pitcher. In fact, during the course of his long career, which saw him pitch for nine teams in both leagues over twenty-one seasons, Hoyt Wilhelm *never* hit another home run. Nor did he ever hit another triple! He got it all out of his system his first two at bats and then concentrated on being one of the great relief pitchers of all time.

For some players, a home run is a great rarity. But for Mike Schmidt, the slugging third baseman of the Philadelphia Phillies, the home run has always been his bread and butter. There is nearly unanimous agreement among baseball people that Schmidt is one of the premier sluggers of the 1970s and '80s. Yet Mike will always remember one particular home run he didn't hit . . . or is it the home run he almost hit . . . or was it the home run he should have hit?

It happened in June of 1974, during Mike's second year with the Phils when he was emerging as a top National League home run hitter. The Phillies were visiting the Houston Astrodome, the first domed stadium in baseball, and in his first at bat, Mike Schmidt hit one a ton.

At the crack of the bat everyone knew the ball was gone. Centerfielder Cesar Cedeño, one of the best fly-chasers in the league, didn't even move. It was just a question of how far into the centerfield seats the ball would travel. But one thing went wrong. The Astrodome, billed as the Eighth Wonder of the World, got in the way.

The ball was already some 300 feet from home plate and about 117 feet high when it suddenly slammed smack into a public address speaker that was suspended from the Astrodome roof. Instead of traveling into the seats, the ball came straight down and landed back on the playing field. Under Astrodome ground rules, the ball was still in play. Schmidt had already gone into his home run trot and had just passed first base when the ball landed. He stopped in his tracks and retreated to the bag, his mouth open in disbelief. He had to settle for a single.

Witnesses estimated the ball would have gone more than 500 feet if it hadn't hit the speaker. And those who designed the ballpark figured no hitter was powerful enough to put a ball up there. But Mike Schmidt did it. And because of that speaker, he probably holds the record for the hardest hit single in baseball history.

"I think people will start to realize that I'm around now," was all Schmidt could say. And he was right.

* * *

Though he is approaching 500 home runs for his career, Phillies slugger Mike Schmidt will never forget the one he didn't hit. The mammoth shot at the Houston Astrodome in 1974 never made it out. Instead, it struck a loudspeaker suspended 117 feet over the playing field, a place deemed safe from a batted ball, and the surprised Schmidt had to settle for a single.

While Mike Schmidt might have been robbed of a home run by a loudspeaker, years ago a player once hit a homer because of a stack of misplaced baseballs. It happened in the old Federal League, which was trying to establish itself as a third major league back in 1914. Only one umpire had showed up for the game, so he was calling balls and strikes from behind the pitcher's mound.

Since umpires did not carry a supply of new baseballs in their pockets back then, the fresh balls were placed in a stack beside the ump and behind the pitcher. It didn't take long for that maneuver to backfire. A batter named Grover Land promptly lined a pitch back toward the mound and it connected with the stack of baseballs, scattering them like the balls on a pool table.

Land began circling the bases as the infielders grabbed at the nearest baseball and tried to tag him. The problem was that no one could prove which one was the batted ball and umpire Bill Brennan felt he had no recourse but to rule the hit a home run. It had to be one of the shortest home runs of all time and probably the last time a stack of baseballs was left on the playing field.

Then there was the home run that was, then wasn't, then was again. On July 24, 1983, the New York Yankees were playing the Kansas City Royals at Yankee Stadium. The Yanks had a 4-3 lead in the top of the ninth with their ace reliever, Rich Gossage, on the mound. With two out and one man on, George Brett, the Royals' top hitter was at the plate.

In a classic confrontation, Brett picked out a Gossage fastball and took it downtown, smashing a two-run homer to give K.C. a 5-4 lead. But wait a minute! Seconds after a smiling Brett trotted across home plate, Yankee manager Billy Martin was out of the dugout, showing plate umpire Tim McClelland something in the rulebook. Then Martin was pointing at Brett's bat.

Many players in recent years have taken to wiping pine tar on their bats, a black, sticky substance that gives them a better grip. Because of that, a rule was made limiting the pine tar to eighteen inches above the knob end of the bat. Martin claimed the pine tar on Brett's bat exceeded the eighteen-inch limit, making the bat illegal.

After examining the bat, the umpire agreed with Martin. He called Brett out, disallowing the homer and declaring the Yanks 4-3 winners. Brett and the Royals went berserk, while Martin and the Yanks looked on. Now they were smiling.

But the Royals weren't finished. They protested to American League president Lee MacPhail. After some consideration, MacPhail ruled in favor of the Royals. He said that while the bat was technically illegal, it didn't violate "the spirit of the rules," and the homer counted. The game would have to be finished with the Royals leading, 5-4. The Yanks would have one more at bat.

So the Brett homer was on again. This time the

Kansas City superstar George Brett with his favorite bat, the one that crashed the famous pine tar home run against the Yankees in 1983.

Yanks complained, but to no avail. The completion took a little more than nine minutes as the Yanks went down in order in the bottom of the ninth. People to this day still debate MacPhail's interpretation of the rules and the pine tar game, as it's now called, is a once-in-a-lifetime part of baseball's folklore. But with all the argument and debate, perhaps it was Yankee outfielder Don Baylor who summed it up best. Leaving the field after the completion of the game, Baylor said:

"If I wanted to watch a soap opera, I'd have stayed home and turned on the television."

Mention the name of Babe Ruth and people think only of home runs. After all, he was the Bambino, the Sultan of Swat, the man who blasted sixty homers in 1927 and 714 over his long career. While both those marks have since been broken, the Babe nevertheless remains the greatest symbol of home run power in baseball history.

Then there is the legend of the Babe, the stories about his enormous appetite, his spending, and the way his home runs resurrected the game of baseball after the Black Sox scandal of 1919. There are also stories of how he inspired kids. In a movie about his life, there was a scene in which a handicapped youngster walked after being encouraged by the Babe. Critics said it was pure nonsense.

But there is a story strangely similar to the movie version related by one of the most respected baseball writers of the century. Fred Lieb, who covered big

The Immortal Babe—George Herman Ruth, who inspired so many baseball stories and legends during his illustrious career.

league baseball for more than sixty years, was with the Yankees in the mid 1920s when the team was playing a spring training game in Tampa, Florida. Shortly after the game began, Lieb saw a big black car pull up and park just outside the rightfield foul line. Like other members of the press, Fred Lieb thought the car belonged to some dignitary and forgot about it.

After the game, the Yankee players left the field and ran past the car to reach their bus, which would take the club back to St. Petersburg. A few minutes later, Lieb's wife, Mary, told her husband she had just had a tip from Leo Durocher, then a young player with the Yanks, that if Lieb went over to the black car he would have a whale of a story.

It might not have been as dramatic as in the movies, but it didn't miss by much. When Fred Lieb went over to the car, he found a man and a boy about ten. The man was delirious with joy and had tears running down his face. When he saw the young reporter, he couldn't wait to tell him the news.

"This is the first time in two years that my boy has stood up," he cried. "Look at him standing here!"

He went on to relate how his son had lost his ability to walk and stand two years earlier. Confined to his room, he began idolizing the Babe, collecting photos and clippings, and following the Yankees feverishly. When the father heard the Yanks would be in Tampa, he got special permission to park near the field so his son could be as close to the Babe as possible.

When the players had run past the car on their way to the bus, the Babe had waved into the window and said, "Hello, kid." And just like in the movies, the young boy struggled to his feet to return the greeting. It's an unbelievable story, but a true one.

"I myself saw one of Ruth's miracles," Fred Lieb later wrote, adding that Leo Durocher, who was running to the bus behind the Babe, "later confirmed the entire story."

But that was the Babe. He was capable of most anything on a ballfield, and he performed a few miracles off the field, as well.

As if on-field heroics aren't enough, baseball players from time to time get a strange urge to try something new and different away from the diamond. Back in the early days of the century, Washington Senators' catcher Gabby Street made a surprising announcement. He would try to catch a baseball dropped from the top of the Washington Monument, a 450-foot structure erected in memory of our nation's first president, George Washington.

Until then, Street was best known as the catcher for the Senators' super pitcher, fastballer Walter Johnson, who won more than 400 games in his career. But the day he stood at the foot of the Washington Monument, Street was on his own. He was taking a chance and he knew it. A ball dropped from that height would have tremendous speed when it reached the bottom. A last-second shift in the wind or a slight misjudgment, and Street could be badly hurt . . . or worse.

A friend of the catcher went to the top of the monument with a number of baseballs and began dropping them, one by one. At first, the wind was the enemy. It blew the balls out of reach, or back into the monument, so they bounced away. Finally, they switched to the other side of the structure where the wind wasn't so bad. Now Street had a chance.

His friend dropped another ball and the catcher circled under it, as if it was a high foul pop. It seemed to take forever to come down as Gabby Street moved back and forth, trying to follow the flight of the ball. POP! It finally landed in Street's glove with such force that the catcher staggered and almost fell. But he held on.

Several years later, someone brought up the accomplishment to Street, remarking that they never thought it could be done.

"Heck, it was easy," Street answered quickly. "You forget I spend the summer catching Johnson's fastball every four or five days."

Unfortunately, not all the once-in-a-lifetime happenings in baseball evoke laughter or wonderment. Like all sports, baseball has an element of danger in it. Numerous players down through the years have suffered severe injuries on the diamond. A number of them, like superstar pitchers Dizzy Dean and Sandy Koufax, have seen their careers shortened or ended by injury. But only once in the long history of the game has a player lost his life as the result of an accident on the ballfield.

It happened on August 16, 1920. The New York Yankees were playing the Cleveland Indians at the old Polo Grounds in New York. Both clubs were battling for the American League pennant and emotions were running high. The Yanks were pitching their ace, Carl Mays, a right-handed submarine pitcher who delivered the ball from such a low angle that his knuckles sometimes scraped the ground.

The Indians had a 3-0 lead when their shortstop, Ray Chapman, came up to lead off the fifth inning. Chapman was a right-handed hitter who crouched over the plate. He had worked the count to one and one when Mays delivered a hard submarine pitch that came in high and tight. The ball kept rising toward Chapman's head. Most players make some kind of effort to get out of the way, but for whatever reason, Ray Chapman just froze, and the ball slammed into the side of his head by the temple.

Chapman went down, then got up, as if to start toward first base. Then he collapsed once again. He was rushed to a hospital where he died before the next morning. Many players, as well as the public, tended to blame Mays for the tragedy, claiming he had thrown at Chapman's head intentionally. But one who absolved the pitcher was Chapman's teammate, Hall of Famer Tris Speaker.

"I don't think Mays deliberately threw at Chappie," Speaker said. "There was time for him to duck, but he never moved. Sure, it was a tight pitch, but we're trained to duck when the ball is coming at us."

Carl Mays continued as a top pitcher. He hurled twenty-six wins that year, and eventually won more than 200 games. But even today, he is remembered more as the pitcher who delivered the only fatal pitch in the history of the game.

Chapter 2

HEY, HAVE I GOT A GREAT IDEA!

Like all the other sports, baseball has had its share of innovators, people who have had visions about changing the game. Some of the changes have become permanent, while others have fallen quickly by the wayside. There have also been many short-term promotions, designed to bring fans to the ballpark. Some of these, such as bat day, cap day, and ball day have caught on all around the leagues. Others have been one-shot fiascos, and still others have caused major problems. But whatever the result, these innovations and promotions were all started with the same thought—"Hey, have I got a great idea!"

Ever wonder why baseball umpires signal a strike by raising their right arms, or signal an out by jerking back their right thumbs? Safe, of course, is both hands thrown out to the sides, palms down. Well, it wasn't always that way. There was a time when the ump just shouted the balls and strikes, safe and out calls. It took a player who couldn't hear them to change things around.

His name was William Ellsworth "Dummy" Hoy, and he played in the National League from 1888 to 1902. "Dummy" was an outfielder who compiled a respectable .291 average during his career. But Dummy Hoy had a handicap. He was a deaf mute and, as such, couldn't hear the umpire's calls. Finally, Hoy had the idea of asking the umpire to raise his right arm to indicate a strike. The umps agreed, and from that request came the standard hand signs that are still used today.

Dummy Hoy, incidentally, saw many umpires using the signs he requested. Born in 1862, at the height of the Civil War, he died on December 15, 1961, at the ripe old age of ninety-nine.

Some ideas, like Dummy Hoy's, quickly become a permanent part of the game. Others just come and quickly go. On August 2, 1938, the Brooklyn Dodgers were hosting a doubleheader against the St. Louis Cardinals at Ebbets Field. Imagine the surprise of the Cardinal team when the host Dodgers brought yellow baseballs out onto the field. Someone had the bright idea that a yellow ball would be easier to follow than the conventional white one.

So the game was played with the yellow baseball.

The Dodgers won it, 6-2, but at the start of the second game, the regular white ball was back. The yellow ball never gained support among any of the other clubs in the majors and never appeared again. It was a one-shot idea that didn't work.

Many of baseball's strangest ideas have been designed to lure more fans through the turnstiles. And it doesn't just happen in the majors. The minor leagues are also fertile ground for wacky ideas.

Take, for example, the time this guy walked up to the owner of a minor league team in Grand Rapids, Michigan, and volunteered to be buried alive in a box behind home plate while the game was being played! Hard to believe, right? Well, the incident was witnessed by Stan Wasiak, the longtime manager of the Los Angeles Dodgers' minor league team at Vero Beach, Florida.

It was a bizarre promotional gimmick, all right, but Wasiak remembers it as if it happened yesterday.

"The guy was a Hindu, from India, I think," Wasiak recalls, "and he used to do this to make money. Before the game they dug a hole behind home plate, put the box down, and he got into it. Then they covered the hole with dirt and said, 'Play ball!'"

So both clubs went out there and played nine innings. It's a wonder that the players could concentrate at all, because each time they ran on and off the field, they knew there was a man buried alive just behind the home plate umpire. He didn't even have any air tubes in the box.

"When the game ended, no one left the ballpark," Stan Wasiak remembers. "They were all waiting to see the guy dug up. Sure enough, he got out of the box still alive, but he was a little groggy. He told us later that he had enough air for about two-and-a-half to three hours. I couldn't help wondering what would have happened if the game went into extra innings.

"The guy also told us about being buried one time when water began seeping into the box. He admitted getting scared when that happened. I'll tell you, I wouldn't do something like that for a billion dollars."

Believe it or not, it happened. The guy probably didn't know much about baseball, either. After all, he never got to watch the game.

The man in the box happened back in the 1940s, but publicity stunts and crazy promos have continued at the minor league level. Stan Wasiak remembers back around 1978 when two minor league outfielders, Marv Garrison and Rickey Henderson, raced a horse for 100 yards. And if the name of Rickey Henderson sounds familiar, he's the same guy who later broke the major league record with 130 stolen bases in a season and as of 1986 was starring for the New York Yankees.

"But he couldn't beat the horse," Wasiak says, with a wink. "The horse won, hands down."

Stan Wasiak has yet another strange baseball memory. He recalls in the early 1980s getting a call at Vero Beach from a guy whose stunt was to blow himself up with dynamite around second base. Once he described his act, Vero Beach officials weighed the value of the publicity stunt and finally gave him the go-ahead.

"His name was Boom Boom Costa, something like that," Wasiak remembers, "and sure enough, he did his act five straight days at Vero Beach. Before the game he got in a box and it really blew up. All he had for protection was a football helmet. Crazy!"

But the craziness isn't reserved for the minor leagues. Major league owners have always looked for ideas that would either help their teams, possibly change the game, or simply bring more customers into the ballpark.

For example, the function of a major league scoreboard was once simply to give the out-of-town scores. The old, traditional scoreboards were hand operated, with the scores posted by an operator working behind the board. By the 1950s, some scoreboards began to work electronically. Then, in 1960, Bill Veeck, owner of the Chicago White Sox, took the scoreboard to new heights.

One of the most promotional minded of all owners, Veeck installed an exploding scoreboard at Comiskey Park. Whenever a White Sox player hit a home run or when the Sox won a ball game, the scoreboard let loose with a wild fireworks display that delighted the fans.

But not everyone appreciated the innovation. When the board began spewing its fireworks display at the powerful New York Yankees in 1960, the Yanks planned revenge. Led by their manager, Casey Stengel, whose baseball knowledge was matched only by his sense of humor, the Yanks waited until one of their own belted a homer at Comiskey Park. Fittingly, it was slugger Mickey Mantle who rode one out. As the Mick circled the bases, Stengel, Yogi Berra, and several other players lit sparklers and whooped it up from the dugout. Take that, scoreboard, they were saying.

Veeck's scoreboard still does its act today and was a forerunner of the multi-million-dollar boards that are an important part of all the new ballparks built in the 1970s and 1980s.

The Houston Astros and New York Mets were both National League expansion teams in 1962. Then, however, the Astros were known as the Colt 45s. Of course, being expansion clubs and stocked with tired veterans and untried rookies, neither team did very well.

A year later, nothing much had changed. And with the season all but finished, someone in the Colt 45s' publicity office had a bright idea. On September 27, 1963, the Houston club started an all-rookie lineup at Colt Stadium. Club officials figured they had a chance to win with this unusual lineup because the Colt 45s were playing the even less successful Mets.

Unfortunately, the strategy didn't work. Starting pitcher Jay Dahl lasted only three innings and the Mets went on to win easily, 10-3. While Dahl never again appeared in a major league game, some of the other

Houston rookies who played that day went on to successful careers. Baseball fans will easily recognize the names of Rusty Staub, Jerry Grote, Jimmy Wynn, and Joe Morgan. Everyone has to start somewhere.

Bill Veeck tried to start a new trend with a rookie of his own back in 1951. As owner of the hapless St. Louis Browns, Veeck decided to create a little excitement in the midst of another last-place season. On August 19, the Browns were at home entertaining the Detroit Tigers in a doubleheader.

The first game was uneventful enough. Then came the nightcap. In the Browns' half of the first inning, outfielder Frank Saucier was due to lead off. But a pinch hitter appeared out of the St. Louis dugout. Suddenly, everyone in the ballpark stood to get a closer look. It seemed as if the Browns were sending a small boy up to the plate!

The batter was only three feet, seven inches tall, weighed sixty-five pounds, and had the number $1/8$ on his uniform shirt. Plate umpire Ed Hurley called time immediately and demanded an explanation. That's when Browns' manager Zack Taylor came out of the dugout and showed Hurley a major league contract.

Meet Eddie Gaedel, a twenty-six-year-old midget, who had actually signed to play for the Browns. Only Bill Veeck would come up with something like this. Umpire Hurley had no choice but to allow Gaedel to bat. The contract was valid and the three-foot, seven-inch player was a legitimate player.

Eddie Gaedel, batting for the St. Louis Browns against the Detroit Tigers in 1951, was the only midget ever to appear in the big leagues. Browns owner Bill Veeck signed him, and Gaedel drew a walk in his only plate appearance.

Gaedel took his place in the batter's box and went into a deep crouch. The strike zone was reduced to microscopic size and Tiger pitcher Bob Cain couldn't find it. He walked Eddie Gaedel on four pitches, whereupon Manager Taylor sent in a pinch runner.

No one knows whether Veeck intended to use Gaedel as a pinch hitter in future situations where a walk was needed to help win a game. He didn't get the chance. American League president Will Harridge would not approve Gaedel's playing contract, claiming that Gaedel playing for the Browns came under the heading of "conduct detrimental to baseball."

So Eddie Gaedel never appeared in a major league game again, but his name will forever be remembered, thanks once more to master showman Bill Veeck. Gaedel, however, would have preferred to remain with the team.

"I felt like Babe Ruth when I walked out on the field that day," he told reporters.

Bill Veeck had to rank as the king of crazy promotional ideas. Some of them worked beautifully; others backfired. But no matter what ballclub Veeck was involved with, the fans knew he would make it interesting.

Just five days after the Eddie Gaedel incident, Veeck was at it again. For an August 24, 1951, game against the Philadelphia Athletics, Veeck announced that some 1,000 or so fans would be allowed to manage the Browns for one night. The "managers" sat behind the Browns' dugout and were given flash cards saying "yes" and "no." Whenever a decision had to be made, the "managers" were asked and would respond by holding up the flash cards. A quick count would determine what the club would do.

The grandstand managers made two lineup changes and the players they inserted wound up with four runs batted in. When St. Louis starter Ned Garver gave up five hits in the first inning, the club asked the managers if a new pitcher should warm up. The vote was no and Garver settled down to allow just two hits the rest of the way as the Browns won the game, 5-3.

It had to be the only game in major league history where the fans made the key decisions that determined the outcome. Leave it to Bill Veeck.

Stories about Bill Veeck's promotions go on and on. In Cleveland, during the 1948 season, the owner saw a letter in a local newspaper in which a fan named Joe Earley wrote that players shouldn't be the only ones given a special night. Veeck picked up on it and a short time later more than 60,000 fans came to huge Municipal Stadium for "Good Old Joe Earley Night."

The surprised letter writer was presented with a new car and numerous other gifts on the field before the game. Even the fans got gifts that night and the first 20,000 women to enter the stadium were given special orchids flown in from Hawaii. Whenever Bill Veeck did something, he did it big.

Of course, not all Bill Veeck's ideas were so great. In July of 1979, when Veeck owned the White Sox, he got together with a Chicago disc jockey and decided to have a night in which fans could protest against disco music. He would give them a chance to burn disco records in a bonfire out in center field at Comiskey Park. Admission to the game was just ninety-eight cents.

Naturally, more than 50,000 fans showed up and before long they got out of hand. The White Sox were playing a doubleheader against Detroit and the fire was supposed to take place between games. Only it didn't take long for the fans to realize the records they had brought resembled frisbees. Before long, records were flying all over the place, in the stands and out onto the field. The umpires had to stop the game several times to clear the records off the field. Soon firecrackers were exploding and more than just records were being thrown.

Still, between games, the promoters tried to stage the record-burning ceremony. It was a farce. About 7,000 fans surged onto the field and began running wild. More police had to be called to the stadium. Even Veeck himself got on the PA system and urged the fans to clear the field. It didn't work.

The promotion turned out to be a disaster. A number of people were arrested and several hurt. And to top it all off, the umpires decided the second game could not be played under dangerous conditions and forfeited it to Detroit. So, thanks to a bad idea, the Sox even lost a ball game.

That wasn't the only time fans on the field presented a problem. But sometimes the situation stayed under control and was ultimately a fun time. Back in 1935, Cincinnati's Larry MacPhail decided to bring night baseball to the major leagues. He set up lights at Crosley Field in Cincinnati and got permission from the league to schedule seven night games during the season.

It went so well that by the time the sixth game rolled around, MacPhail decided to do a little extra to promote it. The Reds would be playing the St. Louis Cardinals. The colorful Cardinal team was known as the "Gas House Gang." The Cards were also defending world champs and drew big crowds wherever they played.

Already anticipating a big crowd, MacPhail also set up special excursion trains and buses to bring in people from the entire Ohio Valley. By game time there was an overflow crowd at Crosley and they were still coming in. Before play had even started, the fans pushed through the barriers and began ringing the field.

It was an unbelievable sight. People were three and four deep down the foul lines, around the catcher, and behind the outfielders. The fans moved right into the Cincinnati dugout, forcing the players to sit against the backstop. Every time a Cardinal player came to bat a lane had to be opened through the crowd.

As the game started, the situation was becoming dangerous. Players couldn't chase fouls, and any ball hit into the crowd behind the outfielders was an automatic double. The people were pressing so close to home plate that the batters were coming within a few feet of hitting someone in the head. Yet the game continued.

Though it was a wild and unusual way to play a baseball game, the Cardinal players didn't really mind. With characters such as Dizzy Dean, Pepper Martin, Leo Durocher, and Ducky Medwick, the players worked the crowd, joking with the fans all game. Medwick began a running conversation with an attractive blond-haired woman. First they talked, then argued, then talked some more. Then in the eighth inning the blonde suddenly walked toward home plate, grabbed a bat out of the hands of Cincinnati's Babe Herman, and announced that she was going to hit.

The umpires looked at each other as the Cardinal players doubled up with laughter. Dizzy Dean's brother, Paul, was on the mound for the Cards and the woman came up wigwagging the bat and demanding that he pitch. Urged on by his teammates, Paul tossed one up underhanded and she hit a little squibbler right back to him. As if acting by instinct, he threw her out at first and the crowd roared with delight.

As it turned out, the woman was a local nightclub performer named Kitty Burke. She kept telling Medwick that she could hit better than he could and he went along with the stunt. She actually wanted the publicity and not long after was hired by a Cincinnati nightclub that billed her as the only woman ever to come to bat in a big league ball game.

Somehow, the game was completed and the fans left without causing any major problems. In spite of that wild night in Cincinnati, night baseball was on the scene for good, one of baseball's great ideas that worked.

Another constant source of wild ideas was the front office of Charles O. Finley, the flamboyant owner of the Kansas City and Oakland Athletics in the 1960s and

'70s. Finley was the kind of owner who liked to call all the shots and perhaps that explains why he went through managers the way a fish goes through water—quickly and easily.

Yet when Charles Finley moved his team to Oakland in the late 1960s, he built a powerhouse, a club that won five straight American League Western Division titles and three consecutive World Series. It was when Finley's team was losing, both on the field and at the box office in Kansas City in the 1960s, that the owner came up with his craziest promotional ideas.

Perhaps the strangest one was the construction of a "Pennant Porch" in right field at Municipal Stadium in Kansas City. Finley claimed that the dimensions of Yankee Stadium, with its short rightfield fence, gave the New York hitters a big advantage and helped turn the Yanks into a perennial powerhouse.

Finley decided to duplicate the Yankee Stadium dimensions in his own ballpark. He moved the foul pole in right field from 338 feet to 325 feet, which was the league minimum for newer parks. Then he angled the fence toward home plate until it was just 296 feet away, the same as at Yankee Stadium. From there, the fence angled out to right center, duplicating the angle of the fence in New York.

The Pennant Porch stayed up for two exhibition games. Then Commissioner Ford Frick and American League president Joe Cronin ordered it removed. But Finley wasn't finished. He tried to get away with half of a Pennant Porch, then he constructed a bleacher roof that jutted over the field to the 296 foot mark. When that was ordered down, he erected a forty-foot-high screen in right. If he couldn't help his own hitters, he'd put a barrier up for the opposing hitters.

That, too, was ordered down. Baseball officials couldn't let an owner alter the dimensions of his ballpark every time he had a whim. But Charles O. Finley tried. In fact, he would try many things before he finally sold the team and left baseball.

Even when he finally found success in Oakland, Charles Finley continued to try new ideas. In the early 1970s, the Oakland team was full of stars, such as Reggie Jackson, Catfish Hunter, Sal Bando, Bert Campaneris, Vida Blue, Joe Rudi, and Rollie Fingers, but owner Finley always managed to stay in the news.

He introduced colorful, gold and green uniforms. Baseball traditionalists frowned. For years, the home team had worn white and the visitors gray. But Finley persisted, and colorful uniforms soon began appearing all over both leagues. The new uniforms certainly looked better on color television.

Another of his fun promotions was "Mustache Day." Every man coming to the ballpark that day was to have grown a mustache. Finley included his ballplayers in the gimmick and they complied, as did stern manager Dick Williams.

The promotion was not only a success, but the A's players and Manager Williams kept their mustaches and started a trend. In the early days of the game,

The mustache revolution was one of Oakland A's owner Charles O. Finley's most successful promotions. Players and fans alike grew their facial hair for Mustache Day. The A's players made it a trademark and started a trend. Clockwise from top left are third baseman Sal Bando, pitcher Rollie Fingers, and catcher Gene Tenace.

players had often worn big handlebar mustaches. But when the A's grew facial hair in the early 1970s, players had been clean shaven for years. Finley helped reverse the cycle. Today, many players wear mustaches and beards. In fact, one of Finley's own players back then, relief star Rollie Fingers, grew an old-fashioned handlebar mustache, which became his trademark, one he retained long after leaving the A's.

So despite some follies like the Pennant Porch, baseball can say thanks to Charles O. Finley. He did have some lasting ideas.

While many of the crazy promotions are gimmicks to bring fans in to see losing teams, there have been some ideas that have backfired on winning teams as well. By now, baseball teams should have learned a lesson. Don't give away anything that isn't valuable enough for the fans to want to keep. And don't give away anything that can be converted into a missile.

Take the case of the Reggie Bar. When Reggie Jackson came to the New York Yankees as a free agent in 1977, he did a lot of talking, both with his mouth and his bat. After he became a World Series hero that year, he remarked that he ought to have a candy bar named after him. He was referring, perhaps jokingly, to the Baby Ruth candy bar, which many people mistakenly think is named after the great Yankee legend, Babe Ruth.

But a candy manufacturer heard Reggie and took his words to heart. Thus was born the Reggie Bar, a circular-shaped candy with a colorful wrapper. Naturally, the Yankees liked the idea and went along with a promotion the next year that saw a Reggie Bar given away to each paying customer.

Unfortunately, the Reggie Bar was not a bat, cap, ball, or a T-shirt, the kind of giveaway that guarantees the fans taking their free gift home. Not everyone likes candy, and with its circular shape, the Reggie Bar could be converted into an instant frisbee.

You guessed it. The players, grounds crew, and umpires spent most of the game picking up Reggie Bars that were thrown periodically from the stands. And when the original Reggie appeared at the plate or made a catch in the field, the bars really sailed.

It was the last of the Reggie Bar giveaways. In fact, while Reggie continued to be a superstar, the Reggie Bar did not. In a few years it was off the market.

In many ways, baseball is the most traditional of all the sports. Yet in many ways it's the most outlandish. For years, baseball uniforms have been pretty standardized. But every now and then, someone gets an idea to change things.

Take the uniforms. From time to time, teams have decided to take a bold step when it comes to baseball fashion. It undoubtedly began way back in the nineteenth century. For instance, back in 1883 there was another Mets team, the Metropolitans of New York. They lasted for just five years in the old American Association, but the players on the club wore sealskin shoes, something rather unheard of in those days.

Then in 1916, the Brooklyn Dodgers decided to try something new. Some say it was because the crosstown Yankees introduced pinstriped uniforms the year before. Anyway, the Dodgers took the field in checkered uniforms, which seemed to embarrass the players more than anyone. Needless to say, the uniforms were quickly discarded.

It was Charles O. Finley who started the next trend in the early 1970s with the Oakland A's. He introduced colored uniforms. That was one new idea that worked and many teams began to use colors other than the traditional gray and white. Done within reason, it was a positive change. But in 1976, the Chicago White Sox took it one step further.

The Sox owner at the time was none other than Bill Veeck. As usual, he had to be different. On August 8, the Sox took the field decked out in white shirts with blue lettering . . . and navy-blue shorts! It was the first time a baseball club had ever worn shorts, and the White Sox players took a terrible ribbing. The opposing Kansas City Royals collapsed in laughter as did many of the fans.

Though the Sox won the ball game, they lost the fashion show. The shorts were quickly discarded in favor of the standard uniform pants. It was an example of an idea carried too far. Somehow, shorts did not befit major league baseball players. Besides, wearing them could make sliding an extremely painful proposition.

But it will happen again, in some form or other. Sooner or later someone will sit up and say, "Hey, have I got a great idea." So stay tuned. The game's not over yet.

Chapter 3

ONLY ON THE DIAMOND

While baseball isn't the only game in town, it can definitely be the weirdest. Perhaps it's due to the game's long history; or maybe just to its nature. But a glance down memory lane in baseball turns up an abundance of mysterious, strange, and amazing stories that can entertain for hours on end. Some of them happened long ago, some recently. But one thing is certain. They couldn't happen in any other sport. Only on the diamond.

Big Ed Delahanty was one of baseball's earliest superstars. The first and most talented of five Delahanty brothers to make the majors, Big Ed was born in 1867 and played professional baseball from 1888 until 1903. In that time he compiled a .345 lifetime batting average, hitting the coveted .400 mark twice.

Big Ed Delahanty—one of the game's first superstars,
as well as one of its strangest mysteries.

In an era of the dead ball, Big Ed was a slugger who could slam the ball farther than most of the other players of his generation. In July of 1897, he became the second player in history to belt four home runs in one game.

Then in 1902, at the age of thirty-four, Big Ed jumped from Philadelphia of the National League to Washington of the new American League. He was still good enough to be the AL's leading hitter with a .376 mark. The following season, Ed Delahanty was again hitting over .300 and showing little sign of slipping despite his thirty-five years. In June, however, manager Tom Loftus suspended Delahanty for drinking. Big Ed followed the team to Detroit on July 3, but left the ballpark before the game was over. No one can be certain what happened on that fateful day, but baseball historian Robert Smith pieced together this account:

Delahanty wired his wife to meet him in Washington, then boarded a late afternoon train for New York. On board, according to witnesses, Delahanty downed five cocktails. He behaved so boisterously the train's conductor had no choice but to put him off at Fort Erie, Ontario, on the Canadian side of the International Bridge.

Delahanty lurched off in pursuit of the train. On the bridge, according to Smith, a watchman named Kingston saw a figure drop out of sight, through the tracks. Below roared the Niagara River. Delahanty's body was recovered a week later, twenty miles downriver. Big Ed Delahanty's career and life ended suddenly on the International Bridge in one of baseball's strangest mysteries.

An on-field death in Toronto a couple of years ago almost spelled big trouble for New York Yankee star Dave Winfield. The Yanks were visiting Exhibition Stadium in August of 1983 for a series against the Blue Jays. Shortly after the game began, the Yankee outfielders were tossing a warmup ball back and forth before the start of an inning.

Winfield, the leftfielder and one of the league's best players, grabbed the warm-up ball, whirled around, and fired it off the field in the direction of the Yankee bullpen. What he didn't see was a seagull that was walking on the field in foul territory. Wouldn't you know it, the ball scored a bull's-eye, hitting the gull and killing it instantly.

As a batboy gingerly put a towel over the fallen bird and carried it from the field, Winfield put his arms out as if to say, hey, I didn't mean it. But the Toronto fans suddenly acted as if the Yankee slugger had killed the team mascot. They not only began booing but also started throwing all kinds of junk his way.

That wasn't all. After the game, Winfield found himself being placed under arrest. He was charged with cruelty to animals, and under Canadian law faced a possible jail term. It took a $500 bond to spring him so he could leave town.

Fortunately, cooler heads finally prevailed, and within a few days the charges against Winfield were

Graceful Dave Winfield of the New York Yankees is one of the fine defensive outfielders in the game. But Winfield made one errant throw that drew national headlines. While tossing a warmup ball off the field in Toronto, Winfield accidentally struck and killed a seagull, and for a brief time was actually placed under arrest.

dropped. But one thing's for sure. Dave Winfield will probably never throw another practice ball off the field without looking carefully. Very carefully.

As Dave Winfield learned the hard way, you've got to be careful where you throw a baseball. But there was an instance on the diamond when a player knew just where he wanted to throw it. Only he couldn't. Mother Nature wouldn't let him.

It happened at the 1961 All-Star Game. The mid-season classic was being played at Candlestick Park in San Francisco. The park had been opened a year earlier to accommodate the Giants after the team had come to the West Coast from New York in 1958. Leaving the antiquated, rundown Polo Grounds, the club looked forward to playing in its new ballpark.

But Candlestick was built alongside the Bay, and the winds coming off the water often played havoc with everything on the ballfield. When the All-Star Game began it was a hot July afternoon. But by the seventh inning the wind was whipping up. That's when Giants' relief pitcher Stu Miller entered the game for the National League.

Miller was a little guy and threw a variety of off-speed pitches. The wind gusts were actually helping him because the ball was moving more than ever. But then, with a runner on first, the wind really did its thing.

After getting the catcher's sign, Miller came to his set position and started to deliver. But just as he began his motion, a sixty-mile-per-hour gust of wind came across the field and literally blew Stu Miller off the mound! He had to struggle to keep from falling over. Needless to say, he didn't complete his delivery.

The plate umpire had no choice but to call a balk, allowing the runner to advance a base. It was the first balk of Miller's long career, and perhaps the only balk in baseball history called because a pitcher was blown off the mound. After the game, one of Miller's teammates suggested the next time he pitched at Candlestick he wear lead shoes.

It wasn't an ill wind, but an ill-thrown ball that caused an embarrassment to Stan Musial. Stan the Man, one of the most respected and talented ballplayers, proved that anyone can fall victim to a strange or freak play that could only happen on the diamond.

The year was 1959 and the thirty-eight-year-old Musial was approaching the end of a brilliant career that would see him finish with a .331 lifetime batting average and seven National League batting titles, as well as a host of other records. But with all those Hall of Fame credentials, Stan the Man probably remembered a play that happened on June 30, 1959, as well as anything.

St. Louis was playing the Chicago Cubs at Wrigley Field and Musial was at bat in the top of the fourth inning. Stan had worked the count to three and one, when pitcher Bob Anderson threw an inside fastball that the plate umpire called ball four. The pitch also got away from catcher Sammy Taylor and Musial headed for first base. But instead of retrieving the loose ball, catcher Taylor, joined by pitcher Anderson, began arguing with umpire Vic Delmore that the ball had hit Musial's bat, and therefore should be a foul.

Then things began happening quickly. As Musial reached first, several of his teammates, seeing that Taylor hadn't gone after the ball, began yelling at him to run to second. But as Stan took off, third baseman Al Dark ran over and picked up the ball, firing it to shortstop Ernie Banks, who was standing about ten feet to the shortstop side of second base.

Meanwhile, as the argument continued at home plate, umpire Delmore automatically took a new ball out of his pocket and handed it to Taylor. Pitcher Anderson, seeing Musial running to second, grabbed the ball from his catcher and fired toward second. Only his throw was wild and went out into center field.

All Musial saw was a baseball flying out into center, so he got up and started toward third, only to run smack into shortstop Banks, who tagged him with the original ball. If you're totally confused by now, you're not alone. So were the Cardinals, the Cubs, and the umpires.

After another argument, and then a conference between the umps, Musial was ruled out, because he was tagged with the original ball. The error had been made by the plate umpire who put the second ball into play. And while Stan the Man probably didn't realize it then, that one base on balls caused a lot more trouble than any of his 3,630 lifetime hits.

* * *

While Stan Musial had to deal with two baseballs, there recently was a player who had to deal with two teams in one day . . . and got to play for both of them. Joel Youngblood was a popular utility player for the New York Mets in the late 1970s and early 1980s. He had a good stick, a great throwing arm, and could play second, third, and the outfield. A handy guy to have around.

On August 4, 1982, Youngblood was the starting centerfielder as the Mets played host to archrival Chicago. In the third inning, he smacked a solid single off the Cubs' Ferguson Jenkins, driving home two runs. Imagine his surprise a couple of innings later when he was suddenly removed from the game. He was even more surprised to learn the reason for his removal. He was no longer a New York Met!

While the game was in progress, the Mets had completed a trade with the Montreal Expos, and Youngblood was one of the players involved. It would have been easy and certainly understandable if Youngblood had gone home for a day or so to think about what had just happened. But a ballplayer is a ballplayer. Noticing that the Expos were playing in nearby Philadelphia, Youngblood left Shea Stadium and got to Philly as fast as he could.

When he arrived, the game was still going on, so he got a Montreal uniform and went into the dugout. Within minutes, Youngblood found himself in the game, as a sixth inning defensive replacement in the outfield. And when he got a turn at bat shortly afterward, he slapped a single off Philly ace Steve Carlton.

Joel Youngblood must have had a lot to think about that night. He had started a game in New York and wound up the day playing in Philadelphia. Along the way he became the only player in major league history to get base hits for two different teams in one day.

The great Ted Williams never had a chance to get hits for two teams in one day. He spent his entire career with just one team, the Boston Red Sox. But Ted got plenty of hits, many of them memorable ones, like belting a home run his last time at bat in the major leagues in 1960.

Of course, when you hit as many baseballs as Ted Williams, there have to be a few strange and amazing ones. In the late 1940s, the Philadelphia Athletics had a pitcher named Lou Brissie, who had come to the majors after World War II. While in the service, Brissie had seen a great deal of action and was wounded. But he recovered to make it to the majors in 1947.

One day the Athletics' left-hander was facing Williams and gave Ted one he liked. He whipped his powerful bat around, but instead of pulling the ball toward right, hit a sharp line drive right back up the middle. CLANG! The sound was unmistakable. Like the ringing of a bell! But the ball seemed to have struck Brissie on the leg. Everyone in the park wondered what had happened.

The ball had hit Brissie, all right, and it had made a

loud clang. Seems as if the wounded war hero had a metal plate on his leg to protect a war wound. Williams's blast had connected with the plate. Fortunately, Brissie wasn't hurt. He continued to pitch in the majors until 1953, but no one ever rang his bell again.

There was another famous explosion off the Williams bat that is always remembered, even today. It came at the All-Star Game in 1946. Ted was en route to a four-for-four performance, with a pair of homers and five RBIs in a game that was never in doubt. The American League drubbed the National, 12-0. But one of Williams's homers that day would become a legend.

The pitcher was Rip Sewell, a Pittsburgh right-hander good enough to win 143 games in his career, including a pair of 21-game seasons. Sewell was as colorful as he was good, for he had a trick pitch called the eephus. It was a high, lazy floater that arched some fifteen feet above the ground and often plopped through the middle of the strike zone when it finally came back to earth.

Sewell delivered the eephus with the same motion as his fastball, so while it was an obvious gimmick that the fans enjoyed watching, it was also effective. Before the All-Star Game began, Ted had asked Sewell if he would throw him the eephus if they faced each other. Sewell said he would, and Williams, being a student of hitting, immediately sought out some advice. He asked his All-Star teammate, the Yanks' Bill Dickey, how he thought the eephus could be hit.

"By stepping up on it," Dickey said without hesitation.

Sure enough, Sewell got into the game and Ted came up. The pitcher remembers Ted shaking his head, as if to say, "Don't throw it," but Sewell nodded, indicating that he would. On the first pitch, Sewell threw the eephus. Ted stepped up and fouled it off for a strike. The crowd was already going wild, enjoying the action. So Sewell threw another. This one was wide of the plate and Ted watched it for a ball. Still being a pitcher who liked the upper hand, Sewell crossed Ted up and fired a fastball down the middle for strike two. But he couldn't resist another eephus.

This time Ted was ready. He watched the ball floating toward home plate, then took a quick step up in the batter's box and timed it perfectly. The ball took off like it was shot out of a cannon. It rocketed on a line into the rightfield bullpen for a home run. Ted grinned as he circled the bases, the roar of the crowd in his ears. On the mound, Rip Sewell was grinning a little, too.

It might have been a freak pitch, some entertaining trickery, but the eephus wasn't easy to hit. In the ten years that Sewell used it, Ted Williams was the only player ever to hit it out of the park.

A 12-0 score in an All-Star Game, such as the one in 1946, is nothing to be laughed at. The players on the losing team have their pride. But one consolation is that the game doesn't count in the standings. Regular season slaughters hurt even more, and perhaps the all-time hurt occurred on June 8, 1950.

That day, the St. Louis Browns were in Boston for a game against the Red Sox. The Browns were not in a very good mood when they arrived at Fenway Park that morning. They had good reason. The day before the Red Sox had buried them by a 20-4 score. A humiliating defeat like that can work one of two ways. It can make a team angry and hungry for revenge. Or it can leave a club dispirited and ripe to be taken again.

The Red Sox must have wondered which St. Louis team they would see. Well, for an inning and a half they couldn't be sure. The game was scoreless. Then in the bottom of the second the question was answered. The Sox scored eight times, and it opened the floodgates. In the third they scored five more, and in the fourth got seven. By the fifth inning the hitters must have been tired of swinging the bat and running the bases. They only scored a pair, making it a 22-3 game after five innings.

When the smoke cleared, the Red Sox had beaten the Browns, 29-4, the most one-sided victory in major league history. Bobby Doerr had three home runs and eight RBIs. Walt Dropo blasted a pair with seven ribbies, while Ted Williams had two circuit clouts and five runs batted in. Johnny Pesky and Al Zarilla had five hits each in the twenty-eight-hit assault. There were only 5,105 fans in Fenway Park that day, but they got about five games' worth of Red Sox offense in a little more than two-and-a-half hours.

* * *

While lopsided scores are rare, they can still happen today. On June 11, 1985, the New York Mets were at Veterans Memorial Stadium in Philadelphia to face the Phillies. The New Yorkers didn't score in the first, and Philadelphia outfielder Von Hayes led off the home half of the inning against left-hander Tom Gorman. Hayes promptly planted one in the rightfield stands for a leadoff home run. And it didn't stop there.

When Von Hayes came up a second time, it was still the first inning. Now, the bases were loaded and the Philly outfielder was facing right-hander Calvin Schiraldi. Boom! He connected again, this time a grand slammer, making him the first player in baseball history to hit two homers in the first inning of a game.

But Hayes wasn't the only one doing the damage. The Phils had nine runs before the first inning was over, and seven more by the time the Mets got them out in the second. When it was over, Philadelphia had a 26-7 victory and the Mets retreated to lick their wounds.

A further irony was that the New Yorkers had been in a horrible team batting slump. The seven runs represented the most they had scored in over a week. Naturally, local sportscasters picked up on it, several opening their broadcasts by saying something like, "Good news for Mets' fans. The team got seven runs tonight." Then came the bad news. . . .

After the game, Mets' manager Davey Johnson tried to be philosophical. "I hope we learn a lesson from this," he said. "As far as I'm concerned this is a rallying cry. We have to stand up. I'm going to make sure twenty-five players are good and teed off."

Mets' general manager Frank Cashen summed up his feeling by saying, "I just feel like I've been through World War III."

A 26-7 score can make someone think like that. Fortunately it doesn't happen too often, but that's not to say it won't happen again. So managers and general managers, beware!

There are plenty of axioms associated with baseball, rules to help play the game better. But here's one people may not have heard before. If your name is Jones, you'd better keep your baseball shoes polished. It might just help your team win the World Series.

Sound crazy? Not really. It's just one of those amazing stories that can only happen on the diamond. And this one happened twice, some twelve years apart. The first time was in the 1957 World Series between the then Milwaukee Braves and New York Yankees.

The Yanks had a two-games-to-one lead as the clubs were battling it out in game four. After nine innings, the score was tied at four apiece. But in the top of the tenth, the Yanks broke through for the go-ahead run off Milwaukee ace Warren Spahn. A 3-1 lead in games would be tough to overcome, and the Braves had just one at-bat to prevent that from happening.

Spahn was due to lead off, so the Braves sent up a pinch hitter, Vernal "Nippy" Jones, a journeyman player in the final year of his career. Yankee lefty

Tommy Byrne was on the mound and his first pitch was low and inside. Umpire Augie Donatelli called it a ball. But wait a minute. Nippy Jones began to argue. He claimed he was hit by the pitch and should be awarded first base.

When Donatelli failed to change the call, Jones asked for the baseball. He showed the umpire a shoe polish mark on the baseball, which he said occurred when the ball hit his shoe. The ump then reversed his call! Jones was hit, he said. The shoe polish proved it. Despite Yankee pleas, he awarded Jones first.

That play changed the course of the game. Byrne became unnerved and the Braves scored three times, the last two riding home on a two-run Eddie Mathews homer. They won it, 7-5, tied the series, and went on to win in seven games. And to many, the turning point was the polish on Nippy Jones's shoe.

It was a play unlikely to happen ever again. But don't bet on anything in baseball! During the 1969 World Series between the New York Mets and Baltimore Orioles, there was an encore presentation. This time it was the fifth game, the Mets leading, three games to one. But in game five, the Orioles had a 3-0 lead as the Mets leftfielder Cleon Jones led off the bottom of the sixth inning.

Oriole left-hander Dave McNally had been coasting up to that time. But one of his deliveries to Jones was a low, inside curveball that skimmed the dirt. Jones backed off and umpire Lou DiMuro called it a ball. Like Nippy Jones a dozen years earlier, Cleon said the

Mets manager Gil Hodges convinces plate umpire Lou DiMuro that outfielder Cleon Jones was indeed hit by a pitch. Hodges proved his point by showing the ump a shoe-polish scuff on the baseball. The action took place in the fifth game of the 1969 World Series and helped key a Mets victory over Baltimore.

ball hit his shoe. Out came Mets' manager Gil Hodges, who grabbed the ball and proceeded to show DiMuro a smudge of polish. Once again the ump accepted the polished proof and sent Jones to first.

An upset McNally then threw a gopher ball to Donn Clendenon and the Oriole lead was down to 3-2. From there the Mets went on to win the game, 5-3, and the series. And for the second time in twelve years, a smudge of polish off the shoe of a player named Jones had been a turning point.

Baseball players always have a great deal of time on their hands. During road trips they are away from families. It's no wonder that practical jokes are often common among the players.

There are the standard things, like nailing down a pair of shoes, putting strange items in another player's locker, dropping water bags out of hotel windows and setting off smoke bombs. Childish? Maybe. But it's often been said that baseball consists of a group of men playing a boy's game.

One of the most original practical jokes was played by a trainer, Frank Bowman of the Cardinals. The victim was young slugger John Mize, who became one of the top power hitters of the later 1930s and 1940s. Early in his career, the man known as the Big Cat was taking a rigorous spring workout. He began perspiring freely and took his sweatshirt off before continuing.

When Mize wasn't looking, trainer Bowman put a flammable substance on the shirt. Later, when Mize finished and went back to get the doctored shirt, Bowman intervened. He said he suspected Mize had broken training rules by drinking a few beers the night before, and to prove it dropped a lighted match on the sweatshirt. It immediately burst into flames.

"See," Bowman said, "you were sweating out the booze. This proves it."

The flabbergasted Mize couldn't believe it. He looked at the blazing sweatshirt again, then begged the trainer not to say anything about the incident. Bowman agreed as he tried desperately to keep himself from laughing.

Of course, what's sometimes laughable to some isn't very funny to others. Take the case of Bob Buhl, a pitcher for the Milwaukee Braves, Chicago Cubs, and Philadelphia Phillies during a career that lasted fifteen years and saw him win 166 games. Not a bad pitcher.

But pitchers have to hit, too, and that's one thing that Bob Buhl couldn't do. Couldn't do at all. Unbelievably, during his long career, Bob Buhl compiled a lifetime batting average of just .089. But that wasn't even the worst part of it. During the 1962 season, when he started thirty-five games as a pitcher, he failed to get a single hit as a batter, going zero for seventy. Not one hit.

In fact, he had a streak that started in late 1961 and lasted into early 1963 in which he went hitless eighty-eight straight times, a major league record. Maybe others were laughing, but not Bob Buhl.

"I tried it all," Buhl said. "I batted right-handed; I batted left-handed. Nothing worked. Even the few hits I did get were accidental."

Buhl speaks the truth. When he got a base hit to end his zero-for-eighty-eight slump, it was a pop to third which a gust of wind blew toward the outfield. As the shortstop and third baseman converged on it, they tangled and tripped, and the ball dropped in for a hit.

It's really amazing to think that a professional baseball player, whether a pitcher or not, could go to bat nearly 100 times without a base hit. But it's equally amazing to think that a player with only one arm could go to bat in sixty-one different big league games and hit over .200. It's true. It really happened.

The player was Pete Gray, who lost his right arm in a truck accident yet decided to pursue a baseball career just the same. Gray made his decision at a good time. It was the early 1940s, during World War II, and many players were in the armed forces. Major league teams were strapped for talent, and players who normally wouldn't have had a chance made it to the bigs.

By 1944, Pete Gray was playing for Memphis in the Southern Association. Incredibly, he put together a Most Valuable Player season, batting .333 with five home runs and sixty-eight stolen bases. When you realize that he could only swing the bat with one arm, his achievement was amazing. In addition, when he caught a fly ball or picked up a base hit in the outfield, he had

Talent in the big leagues was thin during World War II, when many great players were in service. One of those who got a chance to play then was Pete Gray, who amazingly made it to the majors with just one arm! Gray, hitting here, didn't last long, but that he played at all was a tribute to his courage and athletic ability.

to toss the ball in the air, discard his glove, and catch the ball again before making his throw.

Yet by 1945 the St. Louis Browns decided to give Gray a chance to play in the majors. He appeared in sixty-one games that year, hitting .218. It was obvious that his handicap was too great for him to become a permanent major leaguer. By 1946 the war veterans had returned and there was no more room for marginal players. But when you consider what he accomplished with one arm, Pete Gray has to be classified a great athlete. And it could only happen on the diamond.

* * *

Pete Gray wasn't the only handicapped player to perform in the majors. The same year he played with the Browns, a pitcher named Bert Shepard appeared in one game for the Washington Senators against the Boston Red Sox. Shepard worked five-and-one-third innings in relief, giving up one run and three hits. He struck out a pair of Red Sox batters.

What made it amazing was that Bert Shepard was pitching with an artificial leg! He lost his right leg below the knee when his plane was shot down in World War II. But he had the guts to come back and he made it to the majors for one game.

Another pitcher, Monty Stratton, also pitched pro ball after losing a leg. The difference was that Stratton was already an established big leaguer, having won fifteen games in both 1937 and 1938 for the Chicago White Sox. But an off-season hunting accident cost him his right leg.

Stratton tried to make it back with an artificial leg and actually won eighteen games as late as 1946 for Sherman in the East Texas League. Though he never pitched in the majors again, Stratton's life was so inspiring that it was made into a major motion picture, *The Stratton Story,* with actor James Stewart portraying the ill-fated pitcher.

Baseball players are a superstitious lot. They have been for a long time. Sometimes, the superstitions are simple, like a player being careful not to step on the foul line as he comes on and off the field. Other players won't change or wash certain items of clothing while they're winning or going real good. Still others are superstitious about duplicating their exact movements when they're on a hot streak: the way they walk, what they eat, how they sit on the bench, how they drink from the water cooler. Any deviation, no matter how slight, might break the streak and bring on a slump.

But there has also been a more mystical side to baseball, as well. There have been many stories written about baseball players who somehow acquire super powers and lead their teams to a pennant. Somehow, stories about ballplayers with a touch of the supernatural have always captured the public's fancy. There have been books, motion pictures, and Broadway shows that have utilized this theme down through the years.

Pitchers may be the most superstitious of ballplayers. There have been a number down through the years who have even tried practicing some voodoo rites to try to break out of slumps. Lucky or magic charms are not uncommon, either. The great Satchel Paige always wore a lucky string bracelet on his right wrist when he pitched in the Negro Leagues. After he came to the majors, someone complained about the bracelet being a distraction and the umpire made Satch remove it. Not to be denied, Paige attached the bracelet to his ankle under his uniform where it couldn't be seen. But he wouldn't pitch without it.

The lure of the mystical side of baseball continues. The April 1, 1985, issue of *Sports Illustrated* magazine told the story of the New York Mets giving a secret tryout to a pitcher named Sidd Finch who could throw a baseball upward of 160 miles per hour. The fastest big leaguers only approach 100 miles per hour. In the story, Finch turns his back on baseball to pursue a more mystical life studying far-off religions.

As it turned out, the article was an April Fools' joke and Sidd Finch was a fictitious creation. But it showed once again how people are still taken by stories of baseball players with skills and powers beyond those of mortal men.

In fact, years ago, whenever a slugger would begin threatening Babe Ruth's legendary record of sixty homers in a season, there were stories that it was the Babe's spirit that stopped them. And, indeed, the two players who came closest, Jimmie Foxx and Hank Greenberg, suffered some tough breaks in the final weeks of their seasons. Otherwise, both might have surpassed sixty. Though the Babe was still alive then, he was viewed as such a larger than life character that some people actually did believe it was a kind of mystical presence that kept others from breaking his mark.

Perhaps when Roger Maris finally broke the mark in 1961, the Babe's spirit just figured it was time to let go. His place in baseball history was already secure. You never know. Stranger things have happened in baseball, and will continue to happen as long as the game is played.

Chapter 4

IT TAKES TEAMWORK

It takes teamwork to accomplish many things in baseball. Individual players help a team to win, but no one can do it alone. A team may need its superstars, but it also needs its role players—the relief pitchers, pinch hitters, pinch runners, defensive specialists, spot starters, guys that can step in and do the job when called upon.

And sometimes it takes teamwork for other things, too. Bench clearing brawls involve a whole team. Ballclubs that forge a certain identity do it because of the individual men that make up the team. Even when a ballclub makes a miracle push to a pennant, or conversely, when a club collapses and folds up in the final weeks of a season, it's a team effort. Both good and poor play is often contagious.

The following stories are definitely about teams,

though they don't necessarily involve every single player. But whether it's five, ten, fifteen, or all twenty-five players involved, it takes teamwork . . . or it wouldn't have happened.

Teamwork was the byword of the 1960 World Series between the New York Yankees and Pittsburgh Pirates. But for most of the series, it seemed that each club took turns working as a team. The result was one of the most amazing World Series on record.

As usual, the Bombers had a power-laden lineup, with the likes of Mickey Mantle, Roger Maris, Yogi Berra, Moose Skowron, Elston Howard, and others. In fact, the following year this Yankee team would set a major league record of two hundred and forty home runs, with Maris hitting sixty-one and Mantle fifty-four. So a case could be easily made for this Yankee ballclub being Murderers' Row II.

Only the Pittsburgh club of 1960 wasn't intimidated. They were a group of scrappers and determined to offset Yankee power with their own brand of winning baseball. It turned out to be a great World Series, going the full seven games, and not decided until the ninth inning of the finale. Then, after a seesaw struggle, Pittsburgh second baseman Bill Mazeroski belted a series-winning home run off the Yankees' Ralph Terry.

But that wasn't the strange part of the 1960 World Series. The strange part was how the games were decided. When the Yankees won, they were Murderers'

Bill Mazeroski of the Pirates joyously completes a trip around the bases after his ninth-inning home run won the 1960 World Series for Pittsburgh over the New York Yankees.

Row all over again. They unloaded for scores of 16-3, 10-0, and 12-0 in games two, three, and six. It seemed like total domination. When the games were closer, however, the Pirates won, taking games one, four, and five by scores of 6-4, 3-2, and 5-2.

Then came the seventh game, which was a wild and woolly affair. The Pirates had an early, 4-0 lead, but by the eighth inning the Yankees had bounced back on top, 7-4. It looked over. Only Pittsburgh wouldn't quit. The Bucs rallied for five big runs in the bottom of the eighth to go ahead, 9-7. Now it looked as if they had it. Not yet. The Yanks made one more stand with two in the ninth to tie, but they were only setting the table for Mazeroski's series-winning blast in the bottom of the final frame.

For the seven-game series, the Yankees outscored the Pirates, 55-27, and outhit them, 91-60. They set World Series records for total bases (142), highest team batting average (.338), most runs, most hits, and most runs batted in (54). The Bronx Bombers? Murderers' Row II? Maybe. But there's never an escape from the bottom line. The Yanks lost. With all the runs, all the hits, all the records, they still lost! That's baseball. It certainly can be strange.

It takes teamwork to win, and sometimes it takes teamwork to lose. It also takes teamwork for two major league teams to get into a beanball war. One of the worst ever occurred on August 12, 1984, between the Atlanta Braves and San Diego Padres. Before it ended, thirteen members of both teams were ejected, and a potentially explosive situation had been created.

Things heated up on the very first pitch of the game. The Braves' Pascual Perez hit San Diego's Alan Wiggins and the party was on. In the second inning, Padres' pitcher Ed Whitson threw one behind Perez's head. It was retaliation, no doubt about it. Both teams came out on the field, but cooler heads prevailed, at least for the moment.

But in the fourth, Whitson sent Perez to the ground again. This time the umps tried to cool things down. Whitson was ejected for intentionally throwing at a batter and San Diego manager Dick Williams got bounced for ordering it.

Perez came up again in the fifth and this time relief pitcher Greg Booker threw at him . . . and missed. Consequently, Booker and acting manager Ozzie Virgil were thumbed out. Then in the eighth, Perez came to bat for a fourth time and reliever Craig Lefferts finally nailed him. Obvious, to say the least. The Padres' pitchers were still trying to retaliate for that first pitch of the game. And this time the brawl began in earnest.

Both teams swarmed onto the field for all-out warfare. It was a baseball brawl at its worst. Players were punching and kicking for some ten minutes. Finally, the umpires restored order and ejected Lefferts and Coach Jack Krol, who was acting as manager. But peace and tranquillity didn't last for long. In the ninth inning

A typical basebrawl. The Braves and Padres mix it up during an August 12, 1984 ballgame. As usual, it started with a beanball, and the benches emptied several times before order was restored.

Braves' pitcher Donnie Moore plunked Graig Nettles and out came both teams once more.

By the time the smoke had cleared, the game had deteriorated into a disgrace. Five fans had to be taken away by the police for actually joining the brawl, and police riot squads were dispatched to guard each dugout. When it was over, National League president Chub Feeney fined and suspended a number of players and both managers. The Padres' Williams received the stiffest penalty, a ten-day suspension and $10,000 fine.

Umpire John McSherry summed it all up by saying,

"It was the worst thing I ever saw in my life. The only way I can describe it is pathetic. It probably set baseball back fifty years."

It takes teamwork, even for something like that.

Teamwork doesn't only include the players on a ball-club. It extends to the front office, the people who must deal with personnel, make trades, run the farm system, and build a winner. Once the ballclub is at or near the top, the front office must keep it there. It isn't always easy, and sometimes deals are made that really stretch the imagination. They are downright strange.

Take the New York Mets. In their early days the Mets were known for their futility. Born to expansion in 1962, the club slowly built a powerful pitching staff and surprised the baseball world by winning the National League pennant and World Series in 1969 after finishing ninth the year before.

But even that unexpected success didn't prevent the Mets from making some of the strangest trades in recent years. The classic occurred at the end of the 1971 season. That's when the Mets gave up on Nolan Ryan. Ryan was an erratic fastballer with great strike-out potential, but a pitcher who couldn't always find home plate. All Ryan wanted was regular work, to be left alone in the starting rotation. The Mets wouldn't allow that.

As a spot starter and reliever in the 1969 pennant year, Ryan was 6-3. But the next two seasons he went

7-11 and 10-14. The Mets had seen enough. They traded him to the California Angels of the American League for Jim Fregosi, who had been California's shortstop for a decade. The Mets wanted him as a third baseman.

What happened? Fregosi fizzled, lasting barely two seasons with the Mets and not hitting more than .234, although he did go on to manage several teams, including the Angels and White Sox. Ryan went on to become one of the great pitchers in baseball history. He was right about regular work. Once in the rotation, he became a record-setter. As of 1985, he was baseball's all-time strikeout king, approaching 4,200 for his career. He had pitched a record five no-hitters and won more than 250 ball games. Left alone to pitch, he could have been a mainstay of the Mets' staff all these years. If only they had known.

But the Mets had some precedent for what they had done. Two years earlier, following their World Series success in 1969, they traded a speedy young outfielder named Amos Otis to the Kansas City Royals for another third base candidate, Joe Foy. This trade was almost as bad as the Ryan-Fregosi deal.

Amos Otis became one of the premier centerfielders in the American League, a durable player, outstanding defensively, and a solid hitter. Foy had one dismal season with the Mets and was gone. In addition, the Mets' incumbent centerfielder at the time, Tommie Agee, whom the club preferred to Otis, started losing it at age thirty. By 1973 he was gone and the Mets struggled to find another centerfielder for years. Otis could have been a very successful answer.

The Mets have not been the only club to fall victim to strange, inexplicable trading. As one former manager and general manager said: "You gamble every time you make a trade. You always know what you've got, but you don't always know what you're getting."

While that statement is obviously a true one, it doesn't explain some of the strange trades that have been made over the years. Take it all the way back to the turn of the century, just prior to the 1900 season. The Cincinnati team had just completed a trade they thought would be a blockbuster. It was, all right, only for the other team involved, the New York Giants.

The Giants had agreed to trade a pitcher named Amos Rusie to the Reds for an untried right-hander fresh out of college. His name was Christy Mathewson. Rusie had won 230 games for the Giants over the past decade and was not yet thirty years old. He was considered a superstar. Mathewson was a college player who had never pitched in a big league ball game.

What happened? Simple. Christy Mathewson became one of the greatest pitchers in baseball history, a Hall of Fame immortal and winner of 373 ball games. Amos Rusie is also in the Hall of Fame, but it was for winning those 230 games with the Giants. Traded to the Reds, he never won another big league ball game. Not one. Rusie came up with a bad arm and didn't recover. It was one of those trades that really changed the course of baseball history.

In modern times there have been several trades that have not only turned out one-sided, but have also affected entire teams for long periods of time. Sixty-five years after giving up Christy Mathewson for Amos Rusie, Cincinnati made another trade that was to prove disastrous.

This one came at the conclusion of the 1965 season. That's when Cincinnati decided to unload Frank Robinson, who had been a National League superstar since 1956. But the Reds concluded that the slugging outfielder was "an old thirty" and going downhill, even though he had been the National League's Most Valuable Player just four years earlier in 1961. So they sent Robby to the Baltimore Orioles for veteran pitcher Milt Pappas. What a mistake!

Robinson quickly showed the American League he was still a Most Valuable Player. In 1966, he won the Triple Crown with a .316 average, forty-nine homers, and 122 RBIs. What's more, he led the Orioles to a World Series triumph that year, and went on to help them win three more pennants and another series. The man who was "an old thirty" continued to be a dangerous hitter until he was past his fortieth birthday. His 586 career homers are the fourth best in baseball history and his uniform number—20—was retired by the Orioles.

As for Pappas, he proved little more than a .500 pitcher for the Reds and in two years was traded again.

Cincy would never win on "Let's Make a Deal" with that one.

Another classic trade occurred early in the 1964 season and it's still talked about today. Two years before that the Cubs brought up a young outfielder named Lou Brock. In his first two seasons in Chicago Brock batted .263 and .268 and showed potential as an exciting baserunner. But some fifty games into the 1964 season, Brock was again around the .250 mark and the Cubs soured on him.

They decided to trade him even-up for St. Louis pitcher Ernie Broglio, who had won twenty-one games in 1960 and eighteen in 1963. Broglio was only 3-5 for the Cards when the trade was made, but the Cubs must have been hoping he'd regain his twenty-victory form. Oh, were they wrong . . . and were they wrong about Lou Brock.

Once he joined the Cards, Brock became the catalyst in the team's drive to the National League pennant. He batted .348 the remainder of the season, stole another thirty-three bases, and was a star in the World Series. More than that, he went on to become a record-setting Hall of Fame player and World Series hero in 1967 and 1968. When he retired, Brock had more than 3,000 career hits and more than 900 career stolen bases, the all-time best. His 118 thefts in a season was also a record until Rickey Henderson's 130 broke it. Lou Brock was one of the most exciting players of his generation.

As for Ernie Broglio, he won only four games the

The power and grace of Frank Robinson, the only player to win the Most Valuable Player award in both leagues. Robby was sent from the Reds to the Orioles in one of the most one-sided trades of all time.

rest of the 1964 season as he was saddled with arm problems. In the following two seasons he won a total of three games before retiring from baseball. It's no fault of Broglio's that his arm went bad, but he remains a symbol of one-sided trades that never should have been made. Teamwork, from the front office, at its worst.

Because of the new rules regarding contracts and the ability of players to more or less control their own destinies, crazy and funny trades are not as likely to happen in baseball. Superstars change teams quite often, but only because owners want to get market value before the players become free agents.

But in the old days, strange and wacky trades were often the order of the day. Players were moved around as pawns and often used as barter in non-baseball-related matters. Again, the object was supposed to be to improve the team, but it didn't always work that way.

For example, in January of 1920 the Yankees and Red Sox announced a major deal. The Yanks would be purchasing an outfielder-pitcher by the name of George Herman Ruth. He was twenty-four years old and just coming into his own, beginning to play more outfield than pitch, even though he had been a star pitcher for the Sox in the 1918 World Series. The Yankees bought Ruth for the then staggering sum of $125,000.

The deal improved the Yankees, all right. George Herman Ruth became the mighty Babe and stunned the baseball world with fifty-four home runs in 1920 and fifty-nine the following year. He changed the face of the game and made the Yankees a powerhouse.

But did the sale of Ruth improve the Red Sox? No way. Owner Harry Frazee simply wanted the cash, and not to benefit his baseball team. He was also a theatrical producer and wanted the money to finance his Broadway productions. Not a way to run a ballclub.

And here's one for the books. Cy Young was the winningest pitcher in baseball history, winding up an illustrious career in 1911 with 511 victories. But as a lightly regarded rookie pitching for Canton in 1889, he was sold to Cleveland, where he began his career in earnest the next year. The price of the sale . . . a suit of clothes!

Then there was the Detroit Tigers of 1905. They had their spring training in Augusta, Georgia, and when they broke camp to head north, there wasn't enough money in the till to pay the rent for the facilities.

Shortly after the season began, the Tigers paid the rent. They sent Augusta a young pitcher named Eddie Cicotte. No one thought much of the strange rent payment at the time. But Cicotte resurfaced in Boston in 1908, went to the White Sox four years later, and won more than 200 games before being banned from baseball after the Black Sox scandal of 1919. But back in 1905, Eddie Cicotte meant no more to his team than a way to pay the rent.

And there was still another trade with a future Hall of Fame ballplayer who was swapped for something other than another player. It happened to Robert

"Lefty" Grove, the eventual winner of 300 major league ball games. Grove was still in the minors in the early 1920s, pitching for the Martinsburg, West Virginia, ballclub when Jack Dunn, owner of the Baltimore Orioles, decided he wanted the hard-throwing southpaw.

Baltimore was still a minor league team in those days, but a step closer to the Bigs than Martinsburg. Anyway, Dunn looked for a way to get Grove for his ballclub. That's when he learned that the Martinsburg team still owed money for an outfield fence recently constructed at its ballpark. Being a shrewd wheeler-dealer, Dunn offered Martinsburg a deal. He'd take Lefty Grove and in return pay for the outfield fence.

So a bargain was struck and Lefty Grove went off to Baltimore, where he attracted enough attention to get his eventual ticket to the majors with the Philadelphia Athletics. But early in his career he had the distinction of being the only player in baseball history traded even-up for an outfield fence. It takes real front-office teamwork to do something like that.

Marathon games really take teamwork. As the game drags on, inning after inning, a team has to be good enough not to lose yet not good enough to win. So does the other team, and the game continues . . . and continues . . . and continues. The longest game in big league history was the twenty-six-inning tie between the Brooklyn Dodgers and Boston Braves on May 1,

1920. The game was still deadlocked when it had to be called because of darkness.

Though a tie game leaves fans with mixed emotions, there was a notable feature about baseball's longest marathon game. Both starting pitchers, Joe Oeschger of Boston and Leon Cadore of the Dodgers, went all the way. Neither needed relief for twenty-six innings, a remarkable achievement.

But when it comes to marathon games, the New York Mets have to be the all-time team champion. Leave it to the Mets, a team that has always seemed to create its share of amazing, strange, and funny baseball stories.

On May 31, 1964, the Mets began playing a doubleheader against the San Francisco Giants. Little did anyone realize when they came to the park that day that they wouldn't be going home for more than ten hours. The first game was over in the regulation nine innings, but it took a little more than three hours for the Mets to lose. Then came game two.

It was tied after nine, tied after fifteen, and still tied after twenty. The two clubs continued playing, everyone bone weary. Finally the Giants broke through to score a run in the top of the twenty-third inning. The Mets couldn't match it and the game ended, some seven hours and twenty-three minutes after it started. Coupled with game one, the doubleheader took more than ten and a half hours to complete.

Four years later the Mets were at it again. This time they were playing the Houston Astros and once more the game went into extra innings. This one was score-less and a monument to offensive futility. Inning after inning both the Mets and Astros tried but failed to score a single run. It seemed as if it would never end, and would even top the mark of the old Dodgers and Braves. The fans must have felt as if they were in the Twilight Zone, destined to watch a scoreless baseball game forever. Finally, in the twenty-fourth inning Houston managed to push a run across and the Mets went home losers again, this time by the longest 1-0 score in baseball history.

Then the Mets took a vacation from marathon games until 1974. This time they were matching futility with the St. Louis Cardinals. They even came close to set-ting a new record. The game continued for twenty-five innings, with all twenty-five players on each team get-ting into the action one way or another. When it ended, guess what? The Mets lost again.

In the 1986 Playoffs and World Series, the Mets also starred in marathon ballgames. But this time, they won them!

Winning wasn't a problem for the 1919 Chicago White Sox. The Pale Hose took the American League pennant and were heavy favorites to defeat the Na-tional League Cincinnati Reds in the upcoming World Series. Though no one knew it then, what was about to emerge from the series was perhaps the darkest hour baseball has ever known. And it took teamwork, at least by one-third of the ballclub.

It's incredible to think that a World Series could be "fixed," but that's exactly what happened in 1919. Eight members of the White Sox became involved in a plot to "throw" the series, allowing Cincinnati to win, hopefully without making it look deliberate. The reward was money. Big-time gamblers wanted to make a bundle betting on the underdog Redlegs.

The White Sox owner, Charles Comiskey, was known back then for paying his players as little as possible. That's why some of the players were easy marks for a bribe. The sad part, other than the fix itself, was that it involved several great players who undoubtedly would have made it to the Hall of Fame.

Shoeless Joe Jackson was the best known, one of the great natural hitters of all time. He compiled a .356 lifetime average, third only to Ty Cobb and Rogers Hornsby on the all-time list. In 1911, Shoeless Joe batted .408, and in 1920, his final season in the majors, he hit a rockin' .382.

Another great player was pitcher Eddie Cicotte, winner of 208 games in his career, and author of a sensational 29-7 mark in the ill-fated season of 1919. George "Buck" Weaver was an all-star shortstop and third baseman who batted a career high .333 in his final season of 1920. Lefty Claude Williams was just coming into his own, having won twenty-three in 1919 and twenty-two in 1920.

Four other players were involved. They were Chick Gandil, the first baseman; centerfielder Oscar

"Happy" Felsch, shortstop Charles "Swede" Risberg, and Fred McMullin, a utility infielder.

How can eight players fix a series? It isn't easy. Like most everything else in baseball, it takes teamwork. A hitter just doesn't take that good cut. A pitcher doesn't have his top stuff. A fielder juggles a ball for a split second, or arrives at a base a moment too late. It can be done in a way that's difficult to detect. Only there were already rumors before the series began, especially when a lot of money was bet on underdog Cincinnati.

It was a best-five-of-nine series in 1919, and Eddie Cicotte started the opener. When the White Sox ace was mauled 9-1, the rumors continued to mount. Hugh Fullerton, a Chicago sports writer who was well respected in the baseball community, said after that first game:

"I don't like what I saw out there today. There's something smelly going on."

Cicotte had a 1.82 earned run average in the regular season and had completed thirty-six of his forty starts. An off day like that didn't seem right. When the Reds won the second game 4-2, beating Claude Williams, they had a big 2-0 advantage.

After game two, White Sox owner Comiskey actually went to National League President John Heydler and said that he felt something was wrong, that there was some funny business on the part of his players. But when AL president Ban Johnson heard about Comiskey's statement, he dismissed it quickly.

"That is the yelp of a beaten cur," Johnson said. At the time, Johnson and Comiskey were feuding about other matters.

So the series continued. Rookie Dickie Kerr, who was not in on the fix, pitched the Sox back into it in game three, winning 3-0. Next, Cicotte was due again, and as writer Fred Lieb reported, he was said to have told a fellow fixer, "We've got to look good in losing because we have to think about our 1920 contracts."

This time Cicotte lost by a 2-0 score, with his own fielding blunders leading to the Cincy runs in the fifth. When Claude Williams lost again, 5-0, the Sox were down four games to one, and in an almost hopeless position. Now the series returned to Cincinnati once more.

More stories appeared questioning the caliber of play, but nothing was proven and the odyssey of this strangest of World Series continued. The Reds took a 4-0 lead in game six and looked to end it. Suddenly, though, the Sox fought back and went on to win the game, 5-4, for Dickie Kerr. When Cicotte won the seventh game, 4-1, people began wondering all over again.

Some rumors surfaced that another syndicate of gamblers had come on the scene and now wanted the Sox to win. Others said that except for the so-called leaders, Gandil and Risberg, the Sox' players hadn't gotten the money they were promised. One more Chicago victory and the series would be even at four games each.

Claude Williams was scheduled to pitch the eighth game for the White Sox, and stories later circulated that it would cost him his life if he won. He was told he would be shot right out on the mound.

True or not, observers said Williams pitched like a frightened man. He didn't get through the first inning, and by the time a relief pitcher came in, Cincinnati had a 5-0 lead. They went on to win the game, 10-5, and the World Series, five games to three. Soon after, the real investigation began.

Sox' owner Comiskey offered a $10,000 reward to anyone who could provide information that something crooked had taken place. The investigation continued for months, even after the 1920 season had begun. Finally, the eight players and a number of gamblers were indicted. A jury trial brought in a "not guilty" verdict because of the lack of hard evidence. The players celebrated, figuring they were free and clear.

But that wasn't the case. In November of 1920, baseball had elected its first commissioner, Judge Kenesaw Mountain Landis. And Judge Landis knew that a repetition of the fix could ruin baseball. Despite the not guilty verdict in the courts, he banned the eight players from baseball forever, including Buck Weaver, who knew about the fix but never took a penny in bribes and played hard throughout the series. But because he knew about it and said nothing, the judge considered him guilty. Landis's edict contained the following words:

"Regardless of the verdict of juries, no player that

throws a game, no player that entertains propositions or promises to throw a game, no player that sits in on a conference with a bunch of gamblers in which ways and means of throwing a game are discussed and does not promptly tell his club about it, will ever again play professional baseball."

Besides the tragedy of the Black Sox scandal for the Chicago team and all of baseball, the eight banned players had squandered their careers. The best of them had many productive years left as the 1920 season proved. Jackson hit .382, Weaver .333, Felsch .338, Cicotte won twenty-one games, and Claude Williams won twenty-two. Yet they had contributed a black mark on baseball and had to go.

One of the classic stories of the Black Sox scandal involved a small boy who was a rabid Sox fan. When the eight players were accused of taking money to throw the series, the young boy was supposed to have sought out Shoeless Joe Jackson, looked into his eyes, and uttered a sentence still often quoted today.

"Say it ain't so, Joe."

Alas, it was so. And had it not been for the emergence of a rising young slugger named Babe Ruth in 1920, the Black Sox scandal may indeed have threatened the future of baseball. It was Ruth's dynamic home runs, something unseen up to that time, that brought the fans back and restored their faith in the boys' game that eight grown men had almost destroyed. It's an amazing story, even today.

* * *

On a lighter note, however, there was the Gas House Gang. That was the nickname given the collection of scrapping, hustling, fighting, joking ballplayers who made up the 1934 St. Louis Cardinals. Playing with a style all their own, the Gas House Gang showed just what teamwork could do. That year they won the National League pennant on the last day of the season and went on to become world champs.

But it was the individuals that made up the team that gave the 1934 Cardinals their character and place in history. Pitcher Dizzy Dean was the resident philosopher, who almost always made good on his many boasts. Third baseman Pepper Martin, known as the Wild Horse of the Osage, was the Pete Rose of his day, a hustling ballplayer and the first to use the headfirst slide. Colorful Leo Durocher, who later gained fame as the manager of the Brooklyn Dodgers, New York Giants, Chicago Cubs, and Houston Astros was the shortstop. Hall of Famer Frankie Frisch played second and also managed the team.

Rip Collins was a power-hitting first baseman, and Hall of Famer Joe "Ducky" Medwick patrolled the outfield. He was as quick with his fists as he was with his bat. Dizzy Dean's kid brother, Paul "Daffy" Dean, was also a mound mainstay that year. In fact, before the 1934 season began, Dizzy bragged that "me 'n Paul" would win forty-five games between them. They won forty-nine.

But what about their colorful nickname? The team was in second place for a good part of the season, chasing the New York Giants. Late in the year they began a stretch run and were winning big. Because of the superstitions many ballplayers carry, the Cards didn't want to change anything that might jeopardize their winning streak. One of the things they refused to do was have their uniforms washed.

During a road trip they played on several wet fields. The uniforms got even dirtier. Martin and Frisch were always sliding headfirst and theirs were caked with mud. Most of their caps were bent and twisted. By the time they came into New York to meet the Giants, the club looked like a bunch of bums off the sandlots. As Leo Durocher recalled: "We looked horrible, we knew it, and we gloried in it."

By the time the club left New York, a writer had dubbed them the Gas House Gang, after the sleazy Gas House district in the city. But it was the players themselves who made the name fit.

Many of the Cardinals, like Martin and Dean, were small-town boys who always liked a good time. To them, baseball and all that went with it was one big game. When the club was on the road, they played pranks on each other and on people they'd meet along the way.

Some of the things they did were nothing more than the acts of grown men who were still kids at heart. They would set off smoke bombs, drop water bags on people, and pretend to be firemen. Anything for a laugh. While they often fought among themselves, they would come to the aid of a teammate in a split second.

The Gas House Gang was the personification of team-work in every sense of the word.

And they won, catching the Giants at the end to take the pennant. The World Series that year went the full seven games as the Detroit Tigers gave the Cards all they could handle. But in the end, the Gas House Gang prevailed, and they completed their legendary season as World Champions.

The seventh game was a fitting conclusion. Dizzy Dean predicted he would pitch a shutout in the finale, and while he gave Manager Frisch and his teammates several nervous moments with his zany antics, he made good still another boast and won it, 11-0. In fact, Dizzy and Daffy won two games each in the fall classic, to make the ending even more perfect. The Gas House Gang would have it no other way.

Chapter 5

UTTERLY AMAZING

Baseball has always been considered the national pastime. There have been many games, many players, many pennant races, and many records set and broken down through the years. Yet every once in a while there is an achievement that stands above the rest as amazing. It can be a single event, or an achievement of several years, or even an entire career. But it's something a single player accomplished in his career, or at a point in his career. And even the most diehard baseball fan stands in awe of its greatness.

There are many kinds of these utterly amazing baseball achievements. Let's take a brief look at some of them. And remember, they really happened.

Today, pitchers are not expected to go nine innings. A complete game from a starter is a welcomed bonus, but teams are ready if the starting pitcher falters. There are all kinds of relief specialists—the long man, the middle man, and that most valuable commodity, the short man, the stopper who gets the save. Stoppers like Bruce Sutter, Rollie Fingers, Willie Hernandez, and Dan Quisenberry are as well known today as the top starting pitchers.

But years ago, there were no relief specialists. Pitchers were expected to finish what they started. And they were also expected to pitch a slew of innings without complaint. Take the case of Charles "Old Hoss" Radbourn. In 1884, Old Hoss was one of two pitchers toiling for the New York Giants. When the other pitcher, Charlie Sweeney, left the team in midseason, Old Hoss had to pitch every day. Yes, every day! So that's what he did. Modern-day pitchers would probably get a sore arm just thinking about what Radbourn did in 1884.

Old Hoss started seventy-two times and never came out for a reliever. Not once. He pitched a total of 630 innings and started his team's final thirty-eight games. At one point he won eighteen straight, tossed eleven shutouts, and finished the season with an earned run average of 1.38. His record in 1884 was sixty games won and only twelve lost.

Even more amazing is the fact that a year earlier Old Hoss started seventy-two times and had a 44-23 record. And in the three seasons following 1884, he started forty-nine, fifty-eight, and forty-eight times. So in a period of five years, Old Hoss Radbourn dragged his

Amazing Charles "Old Hoss" Radbourn, who spent
the last half of the 1884 season pitching every day and
then went on to average more than 60 starts per year
for the next three years.

arm out to the mound for 299 starts, averaging one start shy of sixty a year. Whatever happened to sore arms? A pitcher couldn't afford one back then. Now that's utterly amazing.

Some twenty years after Hoss Radbourn's incredible performance, there was still another pitching feat that is still remembered today. During the 1905 season, Christy Mathewson compiled a 31-8 record for the New York Giants. That was surely a great record, but then again, Mathewson was a great pitcher, a future Hall of Famer who would win 373 games during his career. But what was really amazing was his pitching in the World Series that year.

The Giants met the Philadelphia Athletics in the fall classic and won it in five games. Three times Christy Mathewson went to the mound in the series. Three times he came away a winner. And three times he shut the Athletics out! Without a single run. All blanks. In twenty-seven innings, all the Athletics managed off Matty was fourteen hits. It was a performance unmatched ever again in more than eighty years of World Series play.

And speaking of incredible performances, it's hard to match what a journeyman outfielder named James Lamar Rhodes did for the New York Giants in 1954. "Dusty" Rhodes spent seven seasons with the New York and San Francisco Giants from 1952 to 1959. He was always a part-time player, a pinch hitter who had

Giants pitcher Christy Mathewson, who compiled an amazing 31-8 record in 1905, including three World Series shutouts.

great defensive deficiencies. In other words, he couldn't field a lick.

In his seven seasons with the Giants, Dusty Rhodes was a .253 hitter. But in 1954, he was Superman!

That year, he was a pinch hitter with a magic touch. In 164 at bats, he hit fifteen home runs, had fifty RBIs, and batted .341. But more amazing than that was his clutch hitting ability, as the Giants drove toward the National League pennant. Manager Leo Durocher remembered it well.

"Every time we needed a pinch hit to win a ball game, there was Dusty Rhodes to deliver it for us," the manager said.

And like the great basketball player who wants the ball when the game is on the line, Dusty Rhodes wasn't afraid to bring his bat to home plate. Whenever the big hit was needed, he would approach his manager and in his Alabama accent, say, "Ah'm your man, Skip."

But there's more. If you think Dusty Rhodes had a great regular season, just listen to what he did in the World Series that year. Playing against the favored Cleveland Indians, winners of 111 games, the Giants took game one into the tenth inning tied at 2-2. That's when Dusty Rhodes came up to pinch-hit for Monte Irvin with two runners on.

Facing twenty-three-game winner Bob Lemon, Rhodes promptly lined a home run over the rightfield fence to win the game.

The next day the Indians had a 1-0 lead in the fifth behind another twenty-three-game winner, Early

Dusty Rhodes was an incredible pinch hitter for the
New York Giants in 1954. Whenever the Jints needed a
clutch hit, it seemed that Rhodes was there to get it for
them. He continued his great stroke right into the
World Series, where this three-run homer won the first
game in the tenth inning.

Wynn. When the Giants put a pair on in the fifth, Manager Durocher sent Rhodes up again. This time Dusty lined a single to center to tie the game. Before the inning ended the Giants had a 2-1 lead. Then in the seventh, Rhodes, who had stayed in the game, slammed a Wynn knuckler against the facade of the upper deck to make it 3-1, the way it ended.

In contest number three, the Giants had a 1-0 lead against nineteen-game winner Mike Garcia when Durocher used his trump card early. He sent Rhodes up as a pinch hitter in just the third inning. But the bases were loaded and the manager wanted to try to break it open. That's the kind of confidence he had in Dusty Rhodes. Sure enough, Dusty responded with a slashing single to drive home two more runs. The Giants went on to win it, 6-2, setting the stage for a 7-4 victory the next day and a sweep of the series.

All Dusty Rhodes did was get four straight pinch hits and drive home seven runs. It capped a season in which he was absolutely amazing.

Some hitting feats take place over a single season while others take longer to achieve. Both ways can dazzle the imagination. Take the case of Rogers Hornsby, one of the greatest hitters who ever lived. He compiled utterly amazing feats over the short term, such as his record-breaking .424 batting average in 1924. But his long-term achievements are just as titanic, especially his .358 career batting mark. Yet even more impressive is what he accomplished over a five-year period beginning in 1921. For those five seasons, Rogers Hornsby had to be the greatest hitter who ever lived.

To hit .400 for a single season is an awesome feat in itself. The last .400 hitter in the majors was Ted Williams in 1941, and before him Bill Terry in 1930. Rogers Hornsby hit .400 a record-tying three times. In fact, he not only hit .400, he averaged .400 for five full seasons! And for those who aren't sure, a .400 average means two hits in every five trips to the plate.

The Rajah started his five-year spree by hitting .397 in 1921. The following year he had his first .400 season, hitting .401 and also winning the Triple Crown, with forty-two home runs and 152 RBIs. Limited to just 107 games by injuries in 1923, Hornsby "slumped" to a mere .384. But he bounced back with a vengeance in 1924 with his big .424 average. And to show none of it was a fluke, he followed up with a .403 season in 1925, taking another Triple Crown with thirty-nine homers and 143 ribbies to go with his out-of-sight batting average.

For those five seasons, Rogers Hornsby had 1,078 hits in 2,679 at bats for a .402 batting average. A right-handed hitter who stood deep in the batter's box and stepped into the ball, Hornsby could go to all fields and hit with power. He credited his sharp eyesight for his batting prowess and wouldn't even read a book or go to the movies, fearful of eyestrain.

Whatever he did, it worked. Because Rogers Hornsby's batting feats over that five-year period just might be the greatest prolonged hitting performance baseball has ever seen.

It's difficult to talk about the hitting of Rogers Hornsby without mentioning the man with whom he is often compared, the great Tyrus Raymond Cobb. Ty, of course, was the complete player of the early days, a ferocious competitor who would do anything to win. He is still considered by many the greatest player of all time.

Cobb, of course, set and still holds many records. His name was in the news in 1985 as Cincinnati's Pete Rose attempted (and ultimately succeeded) to break his lifetime record of 4,191 base hits. But of all Cobb's achievements over his twenty-four-year career, perhaps the most memorable was the stranglehold he had on the American League batting title.

In all, Ty won twelve batting crowns, an all-time record by far. Of those, nine came in succession from 1907 through 1915. Imagine that, for a period of nine years, no player in the entire American League could compile a higher season's average than Ty Cobb. He hit over .400 twice in the string, and for a four-year period from 1910 to 1913 averaged .403.

Finally, in 1916, Tris Speaker broke through and won the bat crown with a .386 mark to Ty's .371. But Cobb came right back to win three more in a row. He later had seasons of .389, .401, and .378, in which he didn't win the batting title, but they show the level of play Ty maintained after the age of thirty.

He was one of the greatest, all right. And it's safe to say no one player will ever dominate the batting title again the way Ty Cobb did. It was utterly amazing.

Back to the mound. Another amazing pitching feat that deserves mention took place over a period of fourteen years. It began as a tragic accident, but in a strange twist of fate, it turned out for the best.

The pitcher's name was Mordecai Peter Centennial Brown. He was born in Nyesville, Indiana, way back in 1876. But from the time he arrived in the big leagues with St. Louis in 1903 until he retired in 1916, he was universally known as Three Finger Brown.

Why Three Finger? Simple. Mordecai Brown only had three fingers on his right hand, his pitching hand. That was the result of a farming accident when he was a youngster. But Mordecai still wanted to pitch, and he gripped the ball the only way he could with his thumb and two remaining fingers. The result was a strange hop on the ball, one he probably couldn't have achieved had his hand not been injured.

So Three Finger Brown made the majors, and before he was through won 239 games, including six straight twenty-game seasons. He pitched some epic battles against Christy Mathewson when Brown was a Cub and Matty a Giant. To top it all off, Mordecai Three Finger Brown was eventually elected to baseball's Hall of Fame. And all because a farming accident cost him two fingers off his pitching hand.

* * *

Back in Mordecai Brown's day, medical science wasn't advanced enough to treat serious sports injuries. Brown was lucky he could pitch after his hand injury. Players today depend on the doctors and all the advances in sports medicine to keep them going. Perhaps the most notable example of modern medicine at its best is the case of Tommy John, the man with the bionic arm.

John was a stylish left-hander who came up with Cleveland in 1963 as a twenty-year-old rookie. Two years later he went over to the White Sox and became a reliable, if not sensational starter. He had some winning seasons and some losing years. In 1972, he was traded to the L.A. Dodgers, where he seemed to be coming into his own. He had an 11-5 mark, then a career best 16-7 record in 1973 at age thirty. It seemed as if he was a late bloomer, especially when he compiled an impressive 13-3 mark through July 17 of 1974.

But with his sights set on his first twenty-victory campaign, Tommy John saw it all come to a halt. He suffered a severe elbow injury in a game against Montreal, and for a while it looked as if his career was over. He had a ruptured ligament, which years ago could not have been repaired. But in a landmark surgical procedure, Dr. Frank Jobe reconstructed John's arm, placing a tendon from his right forearm into his left elbow.

Because the operation hadn't been done before, Tommy John was told he would recover use of the arm, but pitching was very doubtful. John was determined to

The bionic left arm of Tommy John in action. Doctors rebuilt John's left elbow with history-making surgery that enabled him to be a big winner right into his forties.

prove the doctor wrong. Though he couldn't even grip a baseball at first, he gradually began working the arm back. He sat out all of the 1975 season, but when 1976 arrived, Tommy John was at the Dodgers' training camp at Vero Beach, Florida. His teammates couldn't believe it.

The Dodgers nursed him slowly into the rotation, and when the year ended he was 10-10. No one could believe John had come back. The next year he proved he was no fluke. The operation seemed to give him more of a natural sinker and he became one of the best pitchers in the National League, finishing the 1977 season with a 20-7 record.

"It's a miracle, that's all there is to it," said teammate Bill Russell. Others echoed the thought and began calling Tommy the man with the bionic arm.

Tommy John continued to pitch with success. After the 1978 season he went over to the Yankees and had several oustanding years in New York, winning twenty-two games in 1980. He was still pitching in 1986, some twelve years after his injury and operation. He had already won well over 200 major league games. After his retirement he will be a serious candidate for the Hall of Fame.

A miracle of modern medicine? And an incredible story? Both, for sure. But don't leave out the human element—the determination of Tommy John.

Chapter 6

TOUCHING ALL THE BASES

Many things that happen in baseball can't really be categorized. These are stories that bear retelling because they are unusual and unique. So this final chapter will simply be a mixed bag of some of the funny, strange, and amazing baseball tales that have lived on down the years. So, in essence, we will finish by touching all the bases.

There's an old saying that things aren't always what they seem to be. It's an axiom that applies to baseball as well as anything else. Just ask Norm Miller, an outfielder with the Houston Astros in the late 1960s and early 1970s.

The Astros were playing the Atlanta Braves one day when Miller wound up on third base during a Houston rally. Relief pitcher Cecil Upshaw fired a low, outside fastball and catcher Bob Didier went out to get it. Suddenly, something white was spinning toward the backstop. Third base coach Salty Parker figured it was a passed ball and shouted to Miller to run home.

Thinking the same thing, Miller broke for the plate. Only catcher Didier didn't bother to run after the white object. Instead, he just stood at home plate and tagged the surprised Miller out as he came in. You see, the object that had spun toward the backstop wasn't the ball. It was a small, white plastic cast that Didier had been wearing on an injured finger. Upshaw's pitch had knocked it right off the catcher's hand.

"The most surprised and embarrassed guy in the whole ballpark was Miller," said one of the Braves. "He was a sitting duck and there was nothing he could do about it."

There have been players, too, who weren't quite what they seemed. In the midst of a torrid pennant race in 1957, the Milwaukee Braves called up a twenty-seven-year-old rookie outfielder from their Wichita farm club for the final months of the season. His name was Bob Hazle and he had played in just six big league games two years earlier with Cincinnati, batting a paltry .231.

But for forty-one games in 1957, Bob Hazle was Ty Cobb, Rogers Hornsby, and Ted Williams rolled into one. He hit .403, drove in key runs, and helped the Braves to the National League pennant. Along the way he was given the nickname "Hurricane," and Milwaukee fans thought they had another superstar on their hands.

Oh, were they wrong. Baseball can be a strange game. In the World Series against the Yankees, Hazle lost the magic. He hit just .154 in four games. He would never find it again. In 1958, the Hurricane was nothing more than a light breeze. He batted just .179 in twenty games and then was shipped over to Detroit. There, he did a bit better, getting to .241 in forty-three games.

But the next season Hazle was gone, never to play in the majors again. Strange enough, his tremendous surge with the Braves in 1957 left him with a lifetime .300 average for his short career. In 110 games, Hurricane Hazle hit .310. It just goes to show you what one good year can do.

There have been a number of other players who have started out as if they were headed directly to the Hall of Fame only to derail before anyone could get a good look. Sometimes an injury is the culprit, but other times the player mysteriously loses the magic.

In 1955, the St. Louis Cardinals brought up a nineteen-year-old pitcher named Lindy McDaniel. He appeared in four games that year, and the next season became a budding relief star with a 7-6 record in thirty-nine appearances. The season after that he was mainly a starter and compiled a solid, 15-9 mark.

But that same year, 1957, Lindy wasn't the McDaniel everyone was excited about. The Cards had brought up his eighteen-year-old brother, Von, right out of high school. Von, a right-hander like Lindy, made two brief relief appearances, then started against the Brooklyn Dodgers. He promptly shut the Brooks out on just two hits. Magnificent.

Von continued in the rotation. In his seventh start he was even better, blanking Pittsburgh on a single hit, and he didn't walk a batter. The kid really seemed to have it all. He finished his rookie season with a 7-5 mark and the Cards saw a superstar in their future.

But the next year something was wrong. Von wasn't the same pitcher. His mechanics were all fouled up. He seemed to have lost his pitching motion. Appearing in just two games without a decision, he was returned to the minors. But it was just no use. He couldn't get straightened out down there, either. Whatever he had briefly in 1957 was gone. He would never again appear in the major leagues, and his baseball career was over at age nineteen.

Older brother Lindy, however, became one of the most successful relievers in history, pitching for twenty-one seasons until 1975. His 987 mound appearances were the most ever with the exception of knuckleballer Hoyt Wilhelm. He pitched successfully for five different clubs and won 141 games. Funny things happen in baseball. The McDaniel brothers are a case in point. Lindy who was, and Von, who might have been.

Then there are injuries. Many promising careers have been shortened or ended by unexpected and severe injury. Perhaps the most notable and recent case was that of Dodger pitcher Sandy Koufax. For the last five years of his career, 1962 to 1966, Koufax was as good as any pitcher who ever lived. But an elbow injury led to an arthritic condition, which worsened as the fastballing left-hander continued to win.

Finally, at the end of the 1966 season, in which he had a 27-9 record, 317 strikeouts, and a 1.73 earned run average, Koufax suddenly retired, his injured elbow too painful and the specter of permanent damage too frightening for him to continue pitching.

It's happened to other players, too. But perhaps for the strangest case of injury ruining a career it's necessary to look at Pete Reiser. The Brooklyn Dodgers brought Reiser up as a twenty-one-year-old in 1940, and he seemed to have everything. He became a regular the next season and promptly led the National League in hitting with a .343 batting average. A year later, Pete Reiser was already showing signs of taking his place among the all-time greats of the game.

By July, he was running away with another batting race, hitting over .380 with talk of a .400 season. But in the middle of the month, the National League discovered Pete Reiser's only weakness. It was the outfield fence. He couldn't seem to stop when he was going after a fly ball. The first fence he hit was in St. Louis, and it wrecked his season. While he wasn't out of action that long, his injury took away the edge and his batting average fell to .310 by season's end.

Unfortunately, Reiser didn't learn. He kept running into outfield walls, even after parks began to use warning tracks. Because of injuries he hit only .277 the following year and then was a part-timer until retiring in 1952. Sadly, his list of injuries from collisions with outfield walls reads like a day at the emergency room.

Starting with a number of concussions, plus severe bumps and bruises, Reiser also suffered two broken ankles, a broken right elbow, and severe injuries to his left knee and left leg. The injuries not only shortened his career, but limited his effectiveness as well. His manager at Brooklyn, Leo Durocher, put it this way:

"Pete Reiser might have been the best baseball player I ever saw. He was a switch hitter, had power from both sides, could run fast and throw well. One year early in his career he stole home seven times. He had everything but luck."

The luckiest break Pete Reiser could have received would have been the elimination of all outfield fences. Then he might have been a superstar.

Some superstars, of course, never hit an outfield wall but often act as if they had. For some reason, many of these zany performers were pitchers. Maybe they got that way sitting around between starts, but the tradition surely goes back a long way.

At the turn of the century there was a left-hander named Rube Waddell, good enough to win 191 games during the course of his career and be elected to the Hall of Fame. But besides winning ball games, Rube Waddell did some strange and unpredictable things. One day, for instance, while he was pitching, he tore out of the ballpark to chase a fire engine. When his team took the field for the next inning, Waddell was among the missing. Let's hope he enjoyed watching the fire.

In 1904, while pitching for the Philadelphia Athletics of the new American League, Waddell pulled perhaps his craziest stunt . . . and it helped make him a legend among flaky left-handers. Rube was en route to a twenty-five-win season, so his teammates had a world of confidence in him. When he went into the ninth inning leading Cleveland, 1-0, they figured the A's had it made. But suddenly Rube wavered, and the Indians loaded the bases with nobody out.

As the next batter came up, Rube began gesturing wildly to his outfielders. No one knew exactly what he wanted, but knowing Waddell, they were suspicious. By now, they were yelling at him to pitch, but he refused. He kept gesturing to his outfielders. Finally, someone figured out what he wanted.

Rube Waddell wanted his three outfielders to come in and sit around the pitcher's mound. He refused to throw a ball until they did. Knowing Waddell, it was a matter of taking him out of the game or doing as he requested. So finally they came in and sat. Waddell smiled and went back to work.

And guess what Rube Waddell did with his outfielders sitting around him and the game on the line? He cranked up his fastball and promptly struck out the side!

Continuing in the great tradition of Rube Waddell, there was Vernon "Lefty" Gomez. Winner of 189 games for the New York Yankees between 1930 and 1942, Lefty was another southpaw who would sometimes rather stare at passing airplanes than throw the baseball.

But when the chips were down, Lefty could handle most of the batters in the American League. One player who gave him all kinds of fits was Jimmie Foxx, old Double-X, and one of the most feared sluggers of his time. Asked how he pitched Foxx, Lefty said: "I give him my best pitch and then run to back up third."

Another time, with Foxx up, Gomez shook off the first sign catcher Bill Dickey flashed to him. Then he shook off another, then a third, then the first one all over again. Finally Dickey went out to the mound and told Lefty he had to throw something.

"Let's wait awhile," Lefty said, in dead earnest. "Maybe he'll get a long-distance phone call."

Lefty also occasionally decided to pull his own brand of practical joke at a time it could have easily affected the outcome of the game. His second baseman for many years was Tony Lazzeri, an outstanding fielder who was known as one of the smartest players in the game. One day Lefty was on the mound with the bases loaded and no one out—a dangerous situation.

So Lefty bore down and got the next batter to hit a comebacker to him. It looked like an easy mound-to-home-to-first double play. What did Lefty do? He turned around and threw the ball to Lazzeri, who was standing between first and second. The shocked Lazzeri just stood there with the ball as a run scored and the bases remained loaded. When he demanded an explanation, Gomez just smiled and said: "I've been reading in all the papers what a smart ballplayer you are and how you always know just what to do with the ball. So I just wanted to see what you would do with that one."

Lazzeri just shook his head and returned to second. He should have known better. After all, he was dealing with the unpredictable Vernon "Lefty" Gomez.

There have been other strange characters on the mound over the years. Right-hander Billy Loes, who pitched for the Brooklyn Dodgers in the 1950s, once bobbled a slow bouncer and claimed he "lost it in the sun."

Then there was Bill Lee, who pitched for the Boston Red Sox in the 1970s. His nickname was "Spaceman," and it wasn't for being an astronaut with NASA. Ask Lee a question about anything and he'd give a long, long answer, most of it not even remotely related to the question.

He also trained by going for long runs, five or ten miles, but not on a track or a lonely road. Lee ran through the streets of Boston, because he wanted to mingle with the people. And he often made pit stops at local hangouts to talk to the fans.

A consistent, if not big winner, Lee wore uniform number 37. One year he requested Red Sox management give him number 337. Why, they wanted to know.

"Because if you turn number 337 upside down it spells LEE," he said. "Then if I stand on my head, people will know who I am."

But perhaps the most legendary of the super flakes was Jay Hanna Dean, the man universally known as Dizzy. Diz made the Hall of Fame on his pitching skills, though his career was cut short by an injury suffered in the 1937 All-Star Game. A line drive broke his toe, and when he tried to come back too soon, he altered his pitching motion and hurt his arm. But in his heyday with the St. Louis Cardinals' Gas House Gang, he was as unpredictable as he was talented.

In 1934, Diz pitched the first game of a doubleheader against Brooklyn. He held the Dodgers hitless into the eighth inning and finished with a three-hit shutout. In the second game, his brother Paul pitched a no-hitter. That angered Diz. He wasn't jealous that his brother had thrown a gem. He was fuming at him for something else.

"Why didn't you tell me before?" he hollered at Paul. "If I'd have known you were gonna pitch a no-hitter, I'd have pitched one, too."

Another time in Boston, Diz bet someone he would strike out Vince DiMaggio every time he faced him.

Vince was Joe DiMaggio's older brother, and not quite the same kind of hitter as the Yankee Clipper. Well, Diz got him three straight times, but when Vince came up for a fourth time there were two out in the ninth inning with the tying run on second.

Diz got two quick strikes on DiMaggio, but then Vince hit a high foul pop behind the plate. The Cardinal catcher prepared to catch it when Diz began screaming:

"Drop it! Drop it or you'll never catch me again!"

Startled, the catcher let the ball drop. It could have ended the ball game, and Manager Frank Frisch was so upset he jumped up to pull Diz out of the game. But he jumped so hard that he hit his head on the top of the dugout and staggered back, dazed.

Diz went back to work quickly and, as he used to say, fogged a third strike past DiMaggio to win the game, and his bet. The sum total of the bet he worked so hard to win was all of eighty cents!

But perhaps the best example of the fun-loving Dean came in the 1934 World Series. That was the year of the Gas House Gang, when the Cards won the pennant at season's end and then faced the Detroit Tigers in the series. It went the full seven games, and the brazen Diz calmly predicted he would shut out the Tigers in the finale. He made his prediction even though he would be pitching with just one day's rest.

Sure enough, the Cards rallied early and took a 7-0 lead. That was all Diz needed. He began clowning around on the mound and in the dugout, enjoying every moment of the final game. At one point the Tigers' slugger Hank Greenberg came up. The book on Greenberg was that he killed the high outside pitch. So what did Diz decide to do? Right. Challenge Greenberg high and outside. Greenberg promptly hit a liner that almost took Diz's head off. The next time Hank came up, Diz was ready to do it again until Manager Frisch threatened to take him out of the game.

"You wouldn't take me out while I'm pitching a shutout," Diz protested.

"Lose Greenberg again and you'll find out," Frisch growled.

The thought of leaving the most enjoyable game of his life was too much for Ol' Diz. He promptly struck Greenberg out. Then about the seventh inning Diz called his manager back to the mound.

"Do you think Hubbell's a better pitcher than me?" he asked.

Frisch was puzzled. Carl Hubbell was the great Giants' hurler whose screwball made him a Hall of Famer.

"No, you're better," Frisch said, trying to please his pitcher.

"Well, then if he can throw the screwball, I ought to be able to do it."

So Diz went back to work again. Here it was, the seventh game of the World Series and he decided to experiment with a pitch he had never thrown in his life. Manager Frisch couldn't believe it. But that was Dizzy Dean for you. Despite everything, he won the game,

11-0, and the Cardinals were World Champs. Nothing could have made Diz happier.

One of the tragedies of baseball is that black players were not accepted into the major leagues until Jackie Robinson joined the Brooklyn Dodgers in 1947. The unwritten rule or color line dated back to the nineteenth century. So before 1947, the top black ballplayers had their own teams and leagues. The Negro Leagues, as they were called, produced some of the greatest ballplayers of all time. Perhaps the most amazing was Leroy "Satchel" Paige. Old Satch was a tall, thin right-hander with a blazing fastball and all the other pitches that went with it.

From the time he began hurling in the Negro Leagues back in 1926, Paige set some records that were truly amazing. And whenever he pitched for black all-star teams against white major leaguers, he dazzled them. There's little doubt that Satch was one of the greatest pitchers ever. And there are some who say he would have been the absolute best.

Just listen to some of the amazing things Satchel Paige did with a baseball. For starters, it's estimated that Paige pitched in more than 2,500 ball games. During that time he threw some 100 no-hitters. Pitching for the renowned Kansas City Monarchs in 1941, he started thirty games in thirty days. His strong right arm never seemed to tire.

In the fall of 1934, he led an all-black team against an all-star team led by Dizzy Dean, who had just com-

Still showing classic pitching form at age 59, the legendary Satchel Paige turns one loose against the Red Sox. Ol' Satch came out of retirement to throw three innings for the Kansas City A's against the Bosox in 1965. Though he spent most of his career in the old Negro Leagues, Paige is still considered one of the greatest of all time.

pleted a season of winning thirty games for the Cardinals and leading them to a World Series triumph. The game went thirteen innings. Ol' Diz allowed just one run and struck out fifteen batters. But Old Satch did better than that. He allowed no runs and fanned seventeen!

Satch pitched against many teams of barnstorming major leaguers, beginning in the early 1930s. He pitched against the likes of Babe Ruth and other Hall of Fame players. The reaction was always the same. Satch dazzled them and left them in awe of his immense pitching talents.

In the fall of 1947, at age forty-one, Satch pitched against fireballer Bob Feller and another team of all-stars. He won by an 8-0 score, striking out sixteen, including some of the top major leaguers of the day. That was the same year Jackie Robinson came to the majors, and the following season the Cleveland Indians had a forty-two-year-old rookie named Satchel Paige.

After more than twenty years in the game, Satch had finally made the majors. He may have been only a shell of his former self, but there was still life in the old arm. Used as both a starter and reliever, Satch threw a 5-0 shutout against the White Sox on August 13, allowing just five hits, and on August 20, he pitched a three-hit, 1-0 masterpiece, again over the White Sox. When the year ended, he had a 6-1 record and had helped the Indians win the pennant.

Three years later, he produced a 12-10 record for the St. Louis Browns. At season's end he was forty-six years old. But that wasn't all. In 1965, the Kansas City A's brought Satch out of retirement at age fifty-nine to pitch against the Boston Red Sox. Satch went three innings and gave up just one hit, while striking out one. He still had it, if only for a short burst.

No one will ever know for sure just what Satch's record would have been had he pitched in the big leagues all along. But the man was amazing. And today he is a member of baseball's Hall of Fame.

Hall of Fame players sometimes put on Hall of Fame performances and still finish second best. Though there hasn't been a .400 hitter in the majors since Ted Williams hit .406 in 1941, there have been two players in baseball history who batted .400 and didn't win the batting crown.

In 1911, Shoeless Joe Jackson batted .408 and finished number two. That year the great Ty Cobb compiled a .420 batting average. But Cobb got a taste of the same thing some eleven years later. In 1922, he batted .401 but lost out in the batting race to George Sisler, who had a .420 mark that same year.

Then there was Ken Johnson, a journeyman pitcher who was toiling for Houston in 1964. Pitching against the Cincinnati Reds on April 23, Johnson had it. Oh boy, did he have it, the best stuff of his career. Through eight innings he hadn't yielded a single hit. One more inning and he'd have every pitcher's dream, a no-hit ball game.

So Johnson went back to the mound in the ninth and did it. He completed a no-hitter. There was only one slight problem. He lost! You see, Houston didn't have any runs, either, and in the Cincy ninth, Pete Rose reached second when Johnson fielded his bunt and threw over the first baseman's head for an error. Pete moved to third on a ground out, and then scored when second baseman Nellie Fox made another error.

Meanwhile, Houston was shut out on five hits by veteran Joe Nuxhall. So Ken Johnson became the only pitcher in baseball history to pitch a complete game no-hitter . . . and lose.

There would have been few, if any, no-hitters in baseball if a rule made back in 1887 had continued. That year, bases on balls were counted as hits. But there have been many rule changes since the first set was compiled by Alexander Cartwright in 1845. Looking at some of the old rules makes you wonder if baseball was the same game back then. It wasn't. Seeing it played more than a hundred years ago would be a strange experience, indeed.

Before 1857, for instance, games were decided when one team scored twenty-one runs, or aces, as they were called then. That year, games finally ended after nine innings—unless, of course, they were tied.

In 1858, the pitcher was allowed to take a short run toward the plate before delivering the ball. Called strikes were also started that year.

In 1880, it took eight balls for a batter to draw a walk. That was modified to six in 1884, then to five in 1887, and finally to four in 1889. In 1893, the pitching distance was lengthened to the present-day sixty feet, six inches. Before that, the mound was only fifty feet from home plate. Wouldn't Nolan Ryan and Dwight Gooden have loved that.

Foul bunts were not considered strikes until 1894. And before 1908, pitchers could soil a new ball to make it harder to hit. Then in 1920 so-called freak deliveries were outlawed, including the spitball. Each team was allowed up to two "spitball pitchers" for the 1920 season. Thereafter, none was allowed. Pitchers who relied on the spitter were allowed to continue to throw it, but newcomers couldn't. But the spitball rule and rules against doctoring the baseball have been among the more difficult to enforce. Some pitchers today are still accused of "loading up," and the opposition and umpires are hard pressed to catch them at it.

It was a different game years ago. But some things always remain the same. Pitchers look for every advantage over hitters. Hitters will do anything to get their batting averages up. And managers will do whatever it takes to win. That's baseball.

One thing baseball has always been known for is its nicknames. Everyone knows the famous ones. Ty Cobb was the Georgia Peach, Babe Ruth the Sultan of Swat or the Bambino, Lou Gehrig was the Iron Horse, Ted Williams the Splendid Splinter, Stan Musial The Man,

Willie Mays The Say Hey Kid, Pete Rose is Charlie Hustle, and Rickey Henderson the Man of Steal.

Reading the pages of the *Baseball Encyclopedia,* which lists all the players who have participated in major league baseball, there are some unbelievably strange and funny nicknames. Here is a random sampling of some of the more unusual nicknames from the annals of baseball. They include both famous and obscure players. Only the nicknames are listed, and reading a list like this can make you wonder if real people really had these names. But it's a fun way to do it. So begin.

Ditto, Polo, Snooker, Smiling Jock, Fido, Beauty, Deerfoot, Bald Billy, Cuke, Desperate, Imp, Eagle Eye, Goobers, Buttons, Buckshot, Crab, Oyster, The Mississippi Mudcat, Slewfoot, Goldbrick, Trolley Line, Pongo, Wheels, Crooning Joe, Dut, Cupid, Fidgety Phil, Coaster Joe, Smiling Pete, Scoops, Hooks, Wildfire, Cannonball, Wahoo Sam, Crungy, Squak, Dingle, Tomato Face, Wee Willie, Dauntless Dave.

Coonskin, Crash, Oats, Bullfrog, Ugly, Pickles, Cozy, Turkey Mike, Swampy, Buttermilk Tommy, Steamboat, Mutz, Cherokee, Suds, Monkey, Gink, The Little Steam Engine, Muscles, Spooks, Moon, Tookie, Piano Legs, Boots, Pumpsie, Highpockets, Stubblebeard, Bad News, Granny, Old Reliable, Shovel, Circus Solly, Bootnose, Herky Jerky, The Meal Ticket, Catfish, Handsome Ransom, Baby, Kangaroo.

Roadblock, Nippy, Lanky, Pinky, Wagon Tongue, Old Folks, Kickapoo, Little Eva, The Freshest Man on

Earth, The Human Eyeball, Peanuts, Footsie, Rabbit, Cuddles, The Wild Horse of the Osage, Stretch, Rubberlegs, The Gause Ghost, The Alabama Blossom, Grandma, Foghorn, Tricky, Peach Pie, Yip, Brains, Gimpy, Tarzan, Dandelion, Jack the Giant Killer, The Vulture, Twitch, Preacher, Braggo.

Muddy, Rubberarm, Skabotch, Silk Stocking, Cracker, Admiral, Bear Tracks, Weaser, Blab, Durango Kid, Twinkletoes, Tillie, Socks, The Naugatuck Nugget, Hardrock, Squirrel, Bucketfoot Al, The Singer Throwing Machine, Bosco, The Gray Eagle, Sponge, Powder, Dummy, White Wings, Sloppy, Abba Dabba, Sleepy, Milkman, Cotton Top, Arky, Hippo, Tweet, Whale, Runt, Little Poison, Big Poison, Stormy, Satchelfoot, Possum, Icehouse, Squash, Highball, Black Jack, Snake, Cocoa, Dandy, Bunions, Noodles, and The Toy Cannon.

That's all, folks.

About the Author

BILL GUTMAN has been an avid sports fan ever since he can remember. A freelance writer for fourteen years, he has done profiles and bios of many of today's sports heroes. Although Mr. Gutman likes all sports, he has written mostly about baseball and football. Currently, he lives in Poughquag, New York, with his wife, two step-children, seven dogs, and five birds.

**Fast-paced, action-packed stories—
the ultimate adventure/mystery series!**

COMING SOON . . .
**HAVE YOU SEEN
THE HARDY BOYS LATELY?**

Beginning in April 1987, all-new Hardy Boys mysteries will be available in pocket-sized editions called THE HARDY BOYS CASEFILES.

Frank and Joe Hardy are eighties guys with eighties interests, living in Bayport, U.S.A. Their extracurricular activities include girlfriends, fast-food joints, hanging out at the mall and quad theaters. But computer whiz Frank and the charming, athletic Joe are deep into international intrigue and high-tech drama. The pace of these mysteries just never lets up!

For a sample of the *new* Hardy Boys, turn the page and enjoy excerpts from DEAD ON TARGET and EVIL, INC., the first two books in THE HARDY BOYS CASEFILES.

And don't forget to look for more of the new Hardy Boys and details about a great Hardy Boys contest in April!

THE HARDY BOYS
CASEFILES™

Case #1
Dead on Target

A terrorist bombing sends Frank and Joe on a mission of revenge.

"*GET OUT OF my way, Frank!*" Joe Hardy shoved past his brother, shouting to be heard over the roar of the flames. Straight ahead, a huge fireball rose like a mushroom cloud over the parking lot. Flames shot fifty feet into the air, dropping chunks of wreckage—wreckage that just a moment earlier had been their yellow sedan. "Iola's in there! We've got to get her out!"

Frank stared, his lean face frozen in shock, as his younger brother ran straight for the billowing flames. Then he raced after Joe, catching him in a flying tackle twenty feet away from the blaze. Even at that distance they could feel the heat.

"Do you want to get yourself killed?" Frank yelled, rising to his knees.

Joe remained silent, his blue eyes staring at the wall of flame, his blond hair mussed by the fall.

Frank hauled his brother around, making Joe face him. "She wouldn't have lasted a second," he said, trying to soften the blow. "Face it, Joe."

For an instant, Frank thought the message had gotten through. Joe sagged against the concrete. Then he surged up again, eyes wild. "No! I can save her! Let go!"

Before Joe could get to his feet, Frank tackled him again, sending both of them tumbling along the ground. Joe began struggling, thrashing against his brother's grip. With near-maniacal strength, he broke Frank's hold, then started throwing wild punches at his brother, almost as if he were grateful to have a physical enemy to attack.

Frank blocked the flailing blows, lunging forward to grab Joe again. But a fist pounded through his guard, catching him full in the mouth. Frank flopped on his back, stunned, as his brother lurched to his feet and staggered toward the inferno.

Painfully pulling himself up, Frank wiped something wet from his lips—blood. He sprinted after Joe, blindly snatching at his T-shirt. The fabric tore loose in his hand.

Forcing himself farther into the glare and suffocating heat, Frank managed to get a grip on his brother's arm. Joe didn't even try to shake free. He just pulled both of them closer to the flames.

The air was so hot it scorched Frank's throat as he gasped for breath. He flipped Joe free, throwing him off balance. Then he wrapped one arm around Joe's neck and cocked the other back, flashing in a karate blow. Joe went limp in his brother's arms.

As Frank dragged them both out of danger, he heard the wail of sirens in the distance. We should never have come, he thought, never.

Just an hour before, Joe had jammed the brakes on the car, stopping in front of the mall. "So *this* is why we had to come here," he exclaimed. "They're having a rally! Give me a break, Iola."

"You knew we were working on the campaign." Iola grinned, looking like a little dark-haired pixie. "Would you have come if we'd told you?"

"No way! What do you think, we're going to stand around handing out Walker for President buttons?" Joe scowled at his girlfriend.

"Actually, they're leaflets," Callie Shaw said from the backseat. She leaned forward to peer at herself in the rearview mirror and ran her fingers hastily through her short brown hair.

"So that's what you've got stuck between us!" Frank rapped the cardboard box on the seat.

"I thought you liked Walker," said Callie.

"He's all right," Frank admitted. "He looked good on TV last night, saying we should fight back against terrorists. At least he's not a wimp."

"That antiterrorism thing has gotten a lot of coverage," Iola said. "Besides . . ."

". . . He's cute," Frank cut in, mimicking Iola.

"The most gorgeous politician I've ever seen."

Laughter cleared the air as they pulled into a parking space. "Look, we're not really into passing out pamphlets—or leaflets, or whatever they are," Frank said. "But we will do something to help. We'll beef up your crowd."

"Yeah," Joe grumbled. "It sounds like a real hot afternoon."

The mall was a favorite hangout for Bayport kids—three floors with more than a hundred stores arranged around a huge central well. The Saturday sunshine streamed down from the glass roof to ground level—the Food Floor. But that day, instead of the usual tables for pizzas, burgers, and burritos, the space had been cleared out, except for a band, which was tuning up noisily.

The music blasted up to the roof, echoing in the huge open space. Heads began appearing, staring down, along the safety railings that lined the shopping levels. Still more shoppers gathered on the Food Floor. Callie, Iola, and four other kids circulated through the crowd, handing out leaflets.

The Food Floor was packed with people cheering and applauding. But Frank Hardy backed away, turned off by all the hype. Since he'd lost Joe after about five seconds in the jostling mob, he fought his way to the edges of the crowd, trying to spot him.

Joe was leaning against one of the many pillars supporting the mall. He had a big grin on his face and was talking with a gorgeous blond girl. Frank hurried over to them. But Joe, deep in conversation with his new friend, didn't notice his brother. More importantly, he didn't notice his girlfriend making her way through the crowd.

Frank arrived about two steps behind Iola, who had wrapped one arm around Joe's waist while glaring at the blond. "Oh, uh, hi," said Joe, his grin fading in embarrassment. "This is Val. She just came—"

"I'd love to stay and talk," Iola said, cutting Joe off, "but we have a problem. We're running out of leaflets. The only ones left are on the backseat of your car. Could you help me get them?"

"Right now? We just got here," Joe complained.

"Yeah, and I can see you're really busy," Iola said, looking at Val. "Are you coming?"

Joe hesitated for a moment, looking from Iola to the blond girl. "Okay." His hand fished around in his pocket and came out with his car keys. "I'll be with you in a minute, okay?" He started playing catch with the keys, tossing them in the air as he turned back to Val.

But Iola angrily snatched the keys in midair. Then she rushed off, nearly knocking Frank over.

"Hey, Joe, I've got to talk to you," Frank said, smiling at Val as he took his brother by the elbow. "Excuse us a second." He pulled Joe around the pillar.

"What's going on?" Joe complained. "I can't even start a friendly conversation without everybody jumping on me."

"You know, it's lucky you're so good at picking up girls," said Frank. "Because you sure are tough on the ones you already know."

Joe's face went red. "What are you talking about?"

"You know what I'm talking about. I saw your little trick with the keys there a minute ago. You made Iola look like a real jerk in front of some girl you've been hitting on. Make up your mind, Joe. Is Iola your girlfriend or not?"

Joe seemed to be studying the toes of his running shoes as Frank spoke. "You're right, I guess," he finally muttered. "But I was gonna go! Why did she have to make such a life-and-death deal out of it?"

Frank grinned. "It's your fatal charm, Joe. It stirs up women's passions."

"Very funny." Joe sighed. "So what should I do?"

"Let's go out to the car and give Iola a hand," Frank suggested. "She can't handle that big box all by herself."

He put his head around the pillar and smiled at Val. "Sorry. I have to borrow this guy for a while. We'll be back in a few minutes."

They headed for the nearest exit. The sleek, modern mall decor gave way to painted cinderblocks as they headed down the corridor to the underground parking garages. "We should've caught up to her by now," Joe said as they came to the first row of cars. "She must be really steamed."

He was glancing around for Iola, but the underground lot was a perfect place for hide-and-seek. Every ten feet or so, squat concrete pillars which supported the upper levels rose from the floor, blocking the view. But as the Hardys reached the end of the row of cars, they saw a dark-haired figure marching angrily ahead of them.

"Iola!" Joe called.

Instead of turning around, Iola put on speed.

"Hey, Iola, wait a minute!" Joe picked up his pace, but Iola darted around a pillar. A second later she'd disappeared.

"Calm down," Frank said. "She'll be outside at the car. You can talk to her then."

Joe led the way to the outdoor parking lot, nervously pacing ahead of Frank. "She's really angry," he said as they stepped outside. "I just hope she doesn't—"

The explosion drowned out whatever he was going to say. They ran to the spot where they'd parked their yellow sedan. But the car—and Iola—had erupted in a ball of white-hot flame!

Case #2
Evil, Inc.

When Frank and Joe take on Reynard and Company, they find that murder is business as usual.

THE FRENCH POLICE officer kept his eyes on the two teenagers from the moment they sat down at the outdoor café across the street from the Pompidou Center in Paris.

Those two kids spelled trouble. The cop knew their type. *Les punks* was what the French called them. Both of them had spiky hair; one had dyed his jet black, the other bright green. They wore identical black T-shirts emblazoned with the words *The Poison Pens* in brilliant yellow, doubtless some unpleasant rock group. Their battered, skintight black trousers seemed ready to split at the seams. And their scuffed black leather combat boots looked as if they had gone through a couple of wars. A gold earring gleamed on one earlobe of each boy.

What were they waiting for? the cop wondered. Somebody to mug? Somebody to sell drugs to? He was sure of one thing: the punks were up to no good as they sat waiting and watchful at their table, nursing tiny cups of black coffee. True, one of them looked very interested in any pretty girl who passed by. But when a couple of girls stopped in front of the table, willing to be friendly, the second punk said something sharp to the first, who shrugged a silent apology to the girls. The girls shrugged back and went on their way, leaving the two punks to scan the passing crowd.

The cop wished he could hear their conversation and find out what language they spoke. You couldn't tell kids' nationalities nowadays by their appearance. Teen styles crossed all boundaries, he had decided.

If the cop had been able to hear the two boys, he would have known instantly where they were from.

"Cool it. This is no time to play Casanova," one of them said.

"Aw, come on," the other answered. "So many girls—so little time."

Their voices were as American as apple pie, even if their appearances weren't.

In fact, their voices were the only things about them that even their closest friends back home would have recognized.

"Let's keep our minds on the job," Frank Hardy told his brother.

"Remember what they say about all work and no play," Joe Hardy answered.

"And *you* remember that if we make one wrong move here in Paris," Frank said, "it'll be our last."

Sitting in the summer late-afternoon sunlight at the Café des Nations, Frank was having a hard time keeping Joe's mind on business. He had no sooner made Joe break off a budding friendship with two pretty girls who had stopped in front of their table, when another one appeared. One look at her, and Frank knew that Joe would be hard to discourage.

She looked about eighteen years old. Her pale complexion was flawless and untouched by makeup except for dark shading around her green eyes. Her hair was flaming red, and if it was dyed, it was very well done. She wore a white T-shirt that showed off her slim figure, faded blue jeans that hugged her legs down to her bare ankles, and high-heeled sandals. Joe didn't have to utter a word to say what he thought of her. His eyes said it all: Gorgeous!

Even Frank wasn't exactly eager to get rid of her.

Especially when she leaned toward them, gave them a smile, and said, "Brother, can you spare a million?"

"Sit down," Joe said instantly.

But the girl remained standing. Her gaze flicked toward the policeman who stood watching them.

"Too hot out here in the sun," she said with the faintest of French accents. "I know someplace that's cooler. Come on."

Frank left some change on the table to pay for the coffees, then he and Joe hurried off with the girl.

"What's your name?" Joe asked.

"Denise," she replied. "And which brother are you, Joe or Frank?"

"I'm Joe," Joe said. "The handsome, charming one."

"Where are we going?" asked Frank.

"And that's Frank," Joe added. "The dull, businesslike one."

"Speaking of business," said Denise, "do you have the money?"

"Do you have the goods?" asked Frank.

"*Trust* the young lady," Joe said, putting his arm around her shoulder. "Anyone who looks as good as she does can't be bad."

"First, you answer," Denise said to Frank.

"I've got the money," said Frank.

"Then I've got the goods," said Denise.

The Hardys and Denise were walking through a maze of twisting streets behind the Pompidou Center. Denise glanced over her shoulder each time they turned, making sure they weren't being followed. Finally she seemed satisfied.

"In here," she said, indicating the entranceway to a grime-covered old building.

They entered a dark hallway, and Denise flicked a switch.

"We have to hurry up the stairs," she said. "The light stays on for just sixty seconds."

At the top of the creaking stairs was a steel door, which clearly had been installed to discourage thieves. Denise rapped loudly on it: four raps, a pause, and then two more.

The Hardys heard the sound of a bolt being unfastened and then a voice saying, *"Entrez."*

Denise swung the door open and motioned for Frank and Joe to go in first.

They did.

A man was waiting for them in the center of a shabbily furnished room.

Neither Frank nor Joe could have said what he looked like.

All they could see was what was in his hand.

It was a pistol—and it was pointed directly at them.

And don't miss these other exciting all-new adventures in THE HARDY BOYS CASEFILES

Case #3
Cult of Crime

High in the untamed Adirondack Mountains lurks one of the most fiendish plots Frank and Joe Hardy have ever encountered. On a mission to rescue their good friend Holly from the cult of the lunatic Rajah, the boys unwittingly become the main event in one of the madman's deadly rituals—human sacrifice.

Fleeing from gun-wielding "religious" zealots and riding a danger-infested train through the wilderness, Frank and Joe arrive home to find the worst has happened. The Rajah and his followers have invaded Bayport. As their hometown is about to go up in flames, the boys look to Holly for help. But Holly has plans of her own, and one deadly secret.

Available in May 1987.

Case #4
The Lazarus Plot

Camped out in the Maine woods, the Hardy boys get a real jolt when they glimpse Joe's old girlfriend, Iola Morton. Can it really be the same girl who was blown to bits before their eyes by a terrorist bomb? Frantically searching for her, Frank and Joe are trapped in the lair of the most diabolical team of scientists ever assembled.

Twisting technology to their own ends, the criminals create perfect replicas of the boys. Now the survival of a top-secret government intelligence organization is at stake. Frank and Joe must discover the bizarre truth about Iola and face their doubles alone—before the scientists unleash one final, deadly experiment.

Available in June 1987.

Sports Illustrated

AND ARCHWAY PAPERBACKS

BRING YOU

GREAT MOMENTS IN FOOTBALL AND BASEBALL

<u>Sports Illustrated</u>, America's most widely-read sports magazine, and Archway Paperbacks have joined forces to bring you some of the most exciting and amazing moments in football and baseball.

GREAT MOMENTS IN PRO FOOTBALL
Bill Gutman
Here are the amazing stories of passes that looked impossible, broken records that seemed untouchable and many other spectacular moments.

STRANGE AND AMAZING FOOTBALL STORIES
Bill Gutman
Read about the incredible catches and the bizarre once-in-a-lifetime flukes that make the gridiron the unpredictable place it is.

STRANGE AND AMAZING BASEBALL STORIES
Bill Gutman
Don't miss the zany, unbelievable and mysterious happenings past and present in the world of baseball.

Coming in Spring 1987

GREAT MOMENTS IN BASEBALL
Bill Gutman
As spring training approaches you will be able to enjoy this exciting book full of great performances, close plays and super team efforts.